D0118600

World Myths and Folk Tales

HOLT, RINEHART AND WINSTON

A Harcourt Education Company

Austin • Orlando • Chicago • New York • Toronto • London • San Diego

Staff Credits

EDITORIAL

Vice-President
Mescal Evler

Executive Editor
Patricia McCambridge

Editor
Carolyn Logan

Copyediting: Michael Neibergall, *Copyediting Manager;* Mary Malone, *Copyediting Supervisor;* Elizabeth Dickson, *Senior Copyeditor;* Christine Altgelt, Emily Force, Julia Hu, *Copyeditors*

Project Administration: Marie Price, *Managing Editor;* Lori De La Garza, *Associate Managing Editor;* Janet Jenkins, *Senior Editorial Coordinator;* Christine Degollado, Betty Gabriel, *Editorial Coordinators*

Editorial Permissions: Carrie Jones, *Supervisor of Copyrights & Permissions*

DESIGN

Graphic Services
Kristen Darby, *Director*
Bob Prestwood, *Senior Ancillary Designer*

Image Acquisitions
Curtis Riker, *Director*
Jeannie Taylor, *Photo Research Supervisor*
Rick Benavides, *Photo Researcher*

Cover Design
Dick Metzger, *Design Director*
Gillian Brody, *Art Buyer*

Cover Art: Larry Reinhart/Carole Newman

PRODUCTION

Carol Trammel, *Production Supervisor*
Michael Roche, *Senior Production Coordinator*

MANUFACTURING/INVENTORY

Shirley Cantrell, *Manufacturing Supervisor*
Deborah Hilst, *Inventory Supervisor*

Requests for permission to make copies of any part of the work should be mailed to the following address: Permissions Department, Holt, Rinehart and Winston, 10801 N. MoPac Expressway, Building 3, Austin, Texas 78759-5403.

Acknowledgments and other credits appear on page 217, which is an extension of the copyright page.

HRW is a trademark licensed to Holt, Rinehart and Winston, registered in the United States of America and/or other jurisdictions.

Printed in the United States of America

ISBN 0-03-067542-1

8 9 043 08 07 06

Contents

Contents Organized by Culture

World Myths and Folk Tales

Myths are probably the world's oldest stories. In fact, the very word *myth* comes from a Greek word, *muthos*, which simply means "story." Reading myths takes you back to a time when stories were told around the hearth fires of the people who lived before written history began. Through myths—along with rituals, cave and rock paintings, songs, and prayers—human beings in those ancient times could find meaning and pattern in their lives. Myths explained the great mysteries of life, gave hope and a sense of purpose, and taught cultural values. They helped people to feel in harmony with a world that could be as dangerous and unpredictable as it was beautiful and nurturing.

Myths and folk tales may be considered the foundation of all written literature. Directly or indirectly, all literature—from classic novels to the young adult book you are reading for pleasure—stems from the ancient mythmaker's impulse to tell meaningful stories.

Beginnings and Endings

Every young child goes through a phase of asking, over and over again, "Why?" and "How?" The world of myth is full of stories that explain why things are the way they are and how things began. Many of the great questions people have had about their lives were answered by myths: Why do people die? Why does evil exist? How did various plants, animals, and geographical features come to be? In every culture, origin myths—myths about beginnings—are among the most common kinds of myths. Thus this book begins with the very essence of mythology—the "how and why" stories that explain how things in our everyday lives began.

Deeds of Gods and Heroes

When you read folk tales and myths, you not only go back in time to meet heroes and heroines, you travel the globe and find them in many countries and cultures—ancient Greece and Rome, China, Africa, the Middle East, and the Americas. Like today's real and fictional heroes, the characters in myths and folk tales—the gods and goddesses, heroes and heroines—spark our imaginations and stay in our memories. The marvelous deeds and adventures of these ancient heroes and heroines find their parallels in today's big-budget action-adventure films, television programs, anime, comic books, video games, and even the front pages of our newspapers.

Perils Along the Way

Today's heroes often ride in rockets instead of on winged horses, and their weapons (if any) are more likely to be fashioned by technology experts rather than by cave-dwelling dwarfs. However, heroes of every time and culture must face perils along the way if they journey forth to do what heroes must do. Myth and folk tale heroes are called upon to take up a quest, or journey, just as each human being must journey through life with varying degrees of certainty and uncertainty. The journey is a test of courage, will, and character, and the challenges come in the form of monsters and evil gods, or temptations and inner struggles. As we read of heroes and heroines who face perils along the way, perhaps we can gain some insight into how we might face our own "monsters."

Transformations

If you tried to think of one central theme that tied all myths and folk tales together, that theme might be what the Greeks called *metamorphosis,* or transformation. Myths and folk tales are often about change—about the mystery of one thing becoming something else. For many of us, and certainly for the ancient storytellers, the story of the shape-changer—the character with the ability to take on a completely different form—is a favorite. Tales like the well-known "Beauty and the Beast" and "The Frog Prince" (as well as the Greek myth "Cupid and Psyche" in

this book) tell about two kinds of transformations: the outer transformation of an ugly monster into a handsome prince, and the inner transformation of a young woman's feelings from revulsion to love. These transformation experiences continue today as a major theme in art and literature. Rather than a frog changing into a prince, there is the person who, through some inner struggle, transforms from something monstrous into a person of strength and goodness.

Foolishness and Trickery

If you could indeed go back and join the audience of an ancient storyteller, you would find that many of the tales were of foolishness, of trickery that transforms, of just plain stupidity that leads to wisdom. These stories abound in every culture and country. The trickster—the troublemaker who disobeys authority and turns things upside down—appears in many of these stories. In this book, you will meet some of the most colorful tricksters: the Norse god Loki, the American Indian Coyote, and the African Ananse. In folk tales, foolish behavior often serves to teach lessons, as in the wise fables of Aesop and the teaching tales of Mulla Nasrudin. "Wise fools" help to teach us that wisdom comes in many forms and that things are not always what they seem, as when the foolish "youngest brother" character so common in fairy tales winds up a hero and wins the princess.

An Open Book to the Past

Opening up a book of myths and folk tales is like finding an incredibly old time capsule full of clues about the past. We recognize some of the items in the time capsule but must guess what others were used for and what they meant to the people who used them.

A book of myths and folk tales is not a one-way ticket to the past—it is a passage to understanding today's literature and art. This is because myths and legends were created as a way to explain the mysteries that perplexed people long ago: Who are we? Where did we come from? What really matters to us? These questions are still with us, and today's writers and artists explore these mysteries with the same love and fascination that drove the first storytellers.

CHAPTER 1
Beginnings and Endings

Wise Whys

From ancient times, people have been curious about the "hows and whys" of life, and we're no different today. Whether it's a myth about how volcanoes were created, a bit of trivia about who invented the first electric toaster, or a comic book story presenting the origins of a superhero, we all enjoy tales that explain how and why various things began.

Atomic Origins

In the 1950s and early 1960s, moviegoers were fed on a steady diet of low-budget "creature features"—films that introduced weird, often gigantic, monsters. Giant ants, giant spiders, giant grasshoppers—even a giant human being or two—rampaged across the silver screen. Many of these mutant menaces had one thing in common: Their origins were linked to the ghastly, unpredictable effects of atomic radiation. It's not hard to see where all this "atomic anxiety" came from: It was the era of fallout shelters and the Cold War.

Not surprisingly, the king of the "atomic monsters," Godzilla, was an import from Japan, a country all too familiar with nuclear destruction. *Gojira*, as the original Japanese version was titled, was released in 1954. (*Godzilla*, the American version of the film, came out two years later.) In the film, a nuclear test in the Pacific awakens Godzilla, a dinosaur-like beast, from its underwater slumber. The nuclear exposure makes the

Memorable Quote

"The world is round and the place which may seem like the end may also be only the beginning."

—Ivy Baker Priest,
Parade, February 16, 1958

creature radioactive and full of a destructive rage that it takes out on Tokyo. Over the course of more than forty years and twenty films, this "King of the Monsters" has remained a reminder of a time when gigantic movie monsters symbolized gigantic real-life anxieties.

That's a First!

We can look at just about anything in our daily environment and ask, "Where did that come from?" or "Who invented it?" Sometimes, as we discover, the origins of things that we take for granted came about through sheer accident—as these two stories demonstrate.

- In 1853, at a resort in Saratoga Springs, New York, Native American chef George Crum was faced with a hard-to-please customer. The customer had returned his French fries, complaining that they were too thick and soggy. After several unsuccessful attempts to get the potatoes "just right" for his picky customer, the irritated chef decided to get a bit of revenge, slicing his potatoes so thin that his customer couldn't possibly eat them with a fork. The result? The customer loved the new thin and crispy treat, and the potato chip was born.

- We can thank an ancient Chinese emperor for one of the world's favorite beverages. Legend has it that back in 2737 B.C., Emperor Shen Nung was outdoors, boiling some water in an open kettle. Suddenly he saw that many leaves from a nearby plant had fallen into the open kettle. The emperor was about to scoop out the leaves, but then he noticed something: The boiling water had become a fragrant and enticing brew. Shen Nung taste-tested the result and was delighted to discover the pleasures of freshly brewed tea.

INVESTIGATE: What other "accidental origins" of everyday things can you discover?

In this creation myth from the Onondaga people, an animal is sent into the watery depths to bring up the mud that is used to form the earth.

The Earth on Turtle's Back

MICHAEL J. CADUTO AND JOSEPH BRUCHAC

Before this Earth existed, there was only water. It stretched as far as one could see, and in that water there were birds and animals swimming around. Far above, in the clouds, there was a Skyland. In that Skyland there was a great and beautiful tree. It had four white roots which stretched to each of the sacred directions, and from its branches all kinds of fruits and flowers grew.

There was an ancient chief in the Skyland. His young wife was expecting a child, and one night she dreamed that she saw the Great Tree uprooted. The next morning she told her husband the story.

He nodded as she finished telling her dream. "My wife," he said, "I am sad that you had this dream. It is clearly a dream of great power and, as is our way, when one has such a powerful dream we must do all that we can to make it true. The Great Tree must be uprooted."

Then the Ancient Chief called the young men together and told them that they must pull up the tree. But the roots of

You Need to Know...
The Onondaga people have lived in the area that is the present-day state of New York for over a thousand years. Today they are joined together with four other American Indian tribes in the Iroquois Confederacy. However, it was not always so. The Onondaga tell of a time long ago when these five nations fought brutally against one another. The Creator was saddened and sent a messenger to the warring tribes. The messenger urged the enemies to become friends—to live in peace and to respect one another. When the leaders of all five tribes had embraced the Great Law of Peace, the five nations were united. To symbolize this union, they uprooted a great white pine tree, threw their war weapons into the earth, and planted a new tree. As you read this myth, look for another uprooted tree.

the tree were so deep, so strong, that they could not budge it. At last the Ancient Chief himself came to the tree. He wrapped his arms around it, bent his knees and strained. At last, with one great effort, he uprooted the tree and placed it on its side. Where the tree's roots had gone deep into the Skyland there was now a big hole. The wife of the chief came close and leaned over to look down, grasping the tip of one of the Great Tree's branches to steady her. It seemed as if she saw something down there, far below, glittering like water. She leaned out further to look and, as she leaned, she lost her balance and fell into the hole. Her grasp slipped off the tip of the branch, leaving her with only a handful of seeds as she fell, down, down, down, down.

Far below, in the waters, some of the birds and animals looked up.

"Someone is falling toward us from the sky," said one of the birds.

"We must do something to help her," said another. Then two Swans flew up. They caught the Woman From The Sky between their wide wings. Slowly, they began to bring her down toward the water, where the birds and animals were watching.

"She is not like us," said one of the animals. "Look, she doesn't have webbed feet. I don't think she can live in the water."

Variations on a Theme

Myths about how the world came to be are as varied as the cultures they reflect. However, many of these myths share some important features.

- In Earth-Diver creation myths, an animal or human dives into the watery depths to bring back mud or clay, which is then used to form the earth. The selection you are reading is a good example of this kind of myth.
- In Earth Mother–Sky Father myths, the world is created when a male and female god are separated from one another.
- In Cosmic-Egg creation myths, the earth is formed inside an egg-like universe. The egg is watched over by a supreme being and then opened to reveal a fully formed world.

"What shall we do, then?" said another of the water animals.

"I know," said one of the water birds. "I have heard that there is Earth far below the waters. If we dive down and bring up Earth, then she will have a place to stand."

So the birds and animals decided that someone would have to bring up Earth. One by one they tried.

The Duck dove down first, some say. He swam down and down, far beneath the surface, but could not reach the bottom and floated back up. Then the Beaver tried. He went even deeper, so deep that it was all dark, but he could not reach the bottom, either. The Loon tried, swimming with his

strong wings. He was gone a long long time, but he, too, failed to bring up Earth. Soon it seemed that all had tried and all had failed. Then a small voice spoke.

"I will bring up Earth or die trying."

They looked to see who it was. It was the tiny Muskrat. She dove down and swam and swam. She was not as strong or as swift as the others, but she was determined. She went so deep that it was all dark, and still she swam deeper. She went so deep that her lungs felt ready to burst, but she swam deeper still. At last, just as she was becoming unconscious, she reached out one small paw and grasped at the

Turtle Talk

In his fabled race against the hare, the turtle proves himself a patient and steadfast creature. The same is true for the turtle species. Having changed very little since prehistoric times, the turtle has outlived many of its competitors. This endurance has earned the turtle a place of honor in many cultures around the world.

- In Japan, the turtle symbolizes good fortune and long life.
- In China, the turtle is believed to carry the world on its back. It is also seen as a symbol of life, fertility, and patience.
- In Africa, the turtle represents feminine power. For the Cree, the Iroquois, and other American Indians, the turtle symbolizes the life-giving Earth.

bottom, barely touching it before she floated up, almost dead.

When the other animals saw her break the surface they thought she had failed. Then they saw her right paw was held tightly shut.

"She has the Earth," they said. "Now where can we put it?"

"Place it on my back," said a deep voice. It was the Great Turtle, who had come up from the depths.

They brought the Muskrat over to the Great Turtle and placed her paw against his back. To this day there are marks at the back of the Turtle's shell which were made by Muskrat's paw. The tiny bit of Earth fell on the back of the Turtle. Almost immediately, it began to grow larger and larger and larger until it became the whole world.

Then the two Swans brought the Sky Woman down. She stepped onto the new Earth and opened her hand, letting the seeds fall onto the bare soil. From those seeds the trees and the grass sprang up. Life on Earth had begun.

Read On

Do you want to read more American Indian traditional myths, legends, or stories? Two good places to start are *The Storytelling Stone* by Susan Feldmann (Delta) and *Crow and Weasel* by Barry Lopez (Farrar, Straus & Giroux). Then, find more origin stories in these classics: *How the Whale Became and Other Stories* by Ted Hughes (Scholastic) and *Just So Stories* by Rudyard Kipling (William Morrow).

Fire has the power to warm, to cook, to burn, to destroy. According to this ancient Greek myth, fire also has the power to make men as powerful as the gods. Read on to see how human beings obtained this precious—and powerful—spark of life.

The Creation of Man

OLIVIA E. COOLIDGE

The Greeks have several stories about how man came to be. One declares that he was created in the age of Kronos, or Saturn, who ruled before Zeus. At that time, the legend says, there was no sorrow, toil, sickness, or age. Men lived their lives in plenty and died as though they went to sleep. They tilled no ground, built no cities, killed no living thing, and among them war was unknown. The earth brought forth strawberries, cherries, and ears of wheat for them. Even on the bramble bushes grew berries good to eat. Milk and sweet nectar flowed in rivers for men to drink, and honey dripped from hollow trees. Men lived in caves and thickets, needing little shelter, for the season was always spring.

Another legend declares that Zeus conceived of animals first and he entrusted their creation to Prometheus and Epimetheus, his brother. First, Epimetheus undertook to order all things, but he was a heedless person and soon got into trouble. Finally he was forced to appeal to Prometheus.

> **You Need to Know...**
> Prometheus (prō•mē′thē•əs), the helper of human-kind, and his brother Epimetheus (ep′ə•mē′thē•əs) belonged to a group of beings known in Greek mythology as the Titans. The Titans were the off-spring of the earth and the sky. Sometimes known as the elder gods, these powerful giants ruled the universe for countless ages. Their reign ended when Zeus (zo͞os), the son of the Titan Saturn (also known as Cronus or Kronos), led a rebellion. Upon seizing his father's throne, Zeus banished many of the Titans to the underworld. He then ushered in the reign of a new group of gods known as the Olympians. Prometheus, who sided with Zeus during the war, was not cast out, although Zeus never fully trusted this wise, quick-witted Titan.

"What have you done?" asked Prometheus.

"Down on the earth," answered his brother, "there is a green, grassy clearing, ringed by tall oak trees and shaded by steep slopes from all but the midday sun. There I sat and the animals came to me, while I gave to each the gifts which should be his from this time forward. Air I gave to the birds, seas to the fishes, land to four-footed creatures and the creeping insects, and to some, like the moles, I gave burrows beneath the earth."

▲ Engraving of statue of Zeus at Olympia by Fischer von Erlach.

"That was well done," answered Prometheus. "What else did you do?"

"Strength," said Epimetheus, "I gave to lions and tigers, and the fierce animals of the woods. Size I gave to others like the great whales of the sea. The deer I made swift and timid, and the insects I made tiny that they might escape from sight. I gave warm fur to the great bears and the little squirrels, keen eyes and sharp talons to the birds of prey, tusks to the elephant, hide to the wild boar, sweet songs and bright feathers to the birds. To each I gave some special excellence, that whether large or small, kind or terrible, each might live in his own place, find food, escape enemies, and enjoy the wide world which is his to inhabit."

"All this is very good," said his brother, Prometheus. "You have done well. Wherein lies your trouble?"

"Because I did not think it out beforehand," said the heed-less brother sadly, "I did not count how many animals there were to be before I started giving. Now when I have given all, there comes one last animal for whom I have neither skill nor shape, nor any place to dwell in. Everything has been given already."

"What is this animal," said Prometheus, "who has been forgotten?"

"His name," said Epimetheus, "is Man."

Thus it was that the future of man was left to Prometheus, who was forced to make man different from all other creatures. Therefore he gave him the shape of the gods themselves and the privilege of walking upright as they do. He gave him no special home, but made him ruler over the whole earth, and over the sea and air. Finally, he gave him no special strength or swiftness, but stole a spark from heaven and lighted a heavenly fire within his mind which should teach him to understand, to count, to speak, to remember. Man learned from it how to build cities, tame animals, raise crops, build boats, and do all the things that animals cannot. Prometheus also kindled fire on earth that man might smelt[1] metals and make

Gigantic Words

The Greeks often described the Titans as great, towering beings. Over time, the word *titan* has come to mean "giant." Here are a few other *titan* word cousins.

- The adjective *titanic* means "gigantic." In 1911, this word was also used to name a huge ocean liner—in its time, the largest in existence. The ship was considered unsinkable. However, the *Titanic* was in fact doomed. On its first voyage across the Atlantic, it struck an iceberg and sank.
- The aptly named metal *titanium* was discovered in 1791. In its purest form, titanium is the strongest metal known to man.
- Two prehistoric beasts, the *titanosaur* (a dinosaur) and the *titanotherium* (a giant rhino), were named after the Titans.

_____
1. **smelt** (smelt): melt and refine.

Titan in a Bind

Another Titan, Atlas, fought faithfully for the Titans during their war against the Olympians. After the Titans' defeat, Zeus condemned Atlas to carry upon his back the entire world—not just the earth, but the heavens as well. (The word *atlas* comes from a Greek word meaning "to support.") When early geographers began to put groups of maps together into books, they would decorate the covers with a picture of Atlas and his unfortunate load. Later, in the 1500s, a Flemish geographer actually called his book of maps an atlas. The name for such books, as you know, has stuck.

tools. In fact, from this heavenly fire of Prometheus all man's greatness comes.

Before this time fire was a divine thing and belonged only to the gods. It was one of their greatest treasures, and Zeus would never have given Prometheus permission to use it in the creation of man. Therefore when Prometheus stole it, Zeus was furious indeed. He chained Prometheus to a great, lofty rock, where the sun scorched him by day and the cruel frost tortured him by night. Not content with that, he sent an eagle to tear him, so that, though he could not die, he lived in agony. For many centuries Prometheus hung in torment, but he was wiser than Zeus, and by reason of a secret he had, he forced Zeus in later ages to set him free. By then, also, Zeus had learned that there is more in ruling than power and cruelty. Thus, the two at last were friends.

The gods reigned supreme over human beings, but, like people, they often exhibited petty human emotions. In this story you will see how the mighty Zeus was plagued by his jealousy of mortals—and how this jealousy drove him to seek revenge.

The Coming of Evil

OLIVIA E. COOLIDGE

After the punishment of Prometheus, Zeus planned to take his revenge on man. He could not recall the gift of fire, since it had been given by one of the immortals, but he was not content that man should possess this treasure in peace and become perhaps as great as were the gods themselves. He therefore took counsel with the other gods, and together they made for man a woman. All the gods gave gifts to this new creation. Aphrodite[1] gave her fresh beauty like the spring itself. The goddess Athene dressed her and put on her a garland of flowers and green leaves. She had also a golden diadem beautifully decorated with figures of animals. In her heart Hermes put cunning, deceit, and curiosity. She was named Pandora, which means All-Gifted, since each of the gods had given her something. The last gift was a chest in which there was supposed to be great treasure, but which Pandora was instructed never to

You Need to Know...

In Greek mythology Pandora was the first woman. Before she was created, men walked the earth alone, enjoying what is known as the Golden Age— a life free from illness, labor, and strife. However, all was not peaceful in the Golden Age. Zeus had become jealous of the privileges Prometheus had granted to men. Not only had Prometheus given men the gift of fire, but he had also arranged for them to keep for themselves the best parts of the animals they sacrificed to the gods. The gods, on the other hand, were offered only the bones and the fat. Because Prometheus had tricked Zeus into this arrangement, Zeus was angrier than ever. Bent on revenge, Zeus set about creating evil in the world, embodying it in his most powerful weapon yet—woman.

_____

1. **Aphrodite** (af'rə•dīt'ē).

open. Then Hermes, the Messenger, took the girl and brought her to Epimetheus.

Epimetheus had been warned by his brother to receive no gifts from Zeus, but he was a heedless person, as ever, and Pandora was very lovely. He accepted her, therefore, and for a while they lived together in happiness, for Pandora besides her beauty had been given both wit and charm. Eventually, however, her curiosity got the better of her, and she determined to see for herself what treasure it was that the gods had given her. One day when she was alone, she went over to the corner where her chest lay and cautiously lifted the lid for a peep. The lid flew up out of her hands and knocked her aside, while before her frightened eyes dreadful, shadowy shapes flew out of the box in an endless stream. There were hunger, disease, war, greed, anger, jealousy, toil, and all

▲ *Pandora* by Dante Gabriel Rossetti.

Go Ahead . . . Open It!

Some older Greek myths suggest that Pandora was actually a goddess before she was a human being. In one of these myths, Pandora emerges from an opening in the earth carrying a large earthenware jar, or *pithos*. Declaring herself to be the "Giver of All Gifts," Pandora lifts the jar's lid and produces an abundant variety of gifts: flowering fruit trees, seeds that she spreads over the earth, grapevines, the craft of weaving, plants for dyeing fabrics, minerals, and two flat stones—flint for the making of fire. Next, Pandora turns the jar on its side, and the mortals watch in amazement as her beauty and grace flood the mountainside, along with the valuable gifts of wisdom, curiosity, memory, community, courage, endurance, lovingkindness, and peace. You might say that this earlier version of Pandora is really a kind of female Prometheus.

the griefs and hardships to which man from that day has been subject. Each was terrible in appearance, and as it passed, Pandora saw something of the misery that her thoughtless action had brought on her descendants. At last the stream slackened, and Pandora, who had been paralyzed with fear and horror, found strength to shut her box. The only thing left in it now, however, was the one good gift the gods had put in among so many evil ones. This was hope, and since that time the hope that is in man's heart is the only thing which has made him able to bear the sorrows that Pandora brought upon him.

▲ *Pandora Opens the Box* by Walter Crane.

For many people, the coming of day is comforting and reassuring—much like the embrace of a loving parent. In this myth, the creation of earth is described as a beautiful wake-up call.

Sun Mother Wakes the World

RETOLD BY DIANE WOLKSTEIN

The earth was asleep. The spirits of all living beings were sleeping. No fish swam. No animal stirred. The wind did not whisper. In the sky, Sun Mother was also asleep. In her sleep, a voice whispered to her, "Wake, wake, my child."

Sun Mother opened her eyes. Light appeared.

"My daughter," the voice spoke again. "It is time for you to wake the sleeping earth." Sun Mother stretched and the light became brighter. Swift as a shooting star, Sun Mother sped to the earth. The earth was gray and empty. There was no color. No sound. No movement.

Sun Mother began to travel. With each step she took, grass, plants, and trees sprouted in her footprints. Sun Mother traveled north, south, east, and west, waking all the earth. Then she rested, surrounded by green plants and trees. Again a voice

> **You Need to Know...**
> The Aborigines of today are the descendants of the first people who lived in Australia. The earliest Aborigines probably came to Australia from Asia about sixty thousand years ago. Over time, the Aborigines have developed a complex culture based on a deep respect for nature. The work of creation, they believe, began with their ancestors during a period known as the Dreamtime. Each animal, plant, and landform created during the Dreamtime is seen as a kind of footprint, or clue, that tells about the ancestors' movements in the world. The Aborigines also believe that creation continues with the birth of each new living thing. For this reason, the place of a person's birth, known as his or her Dreaming, is considered sacred. It is, after all, the first gentle call of the Sun Mother to yet another of her beloved creatures.

called to her. "My daughter, it is time for you to go to the dark caves to wake the sleeping animal spirits."

Sun Mother entered a large cave. Light flooded the cave. The witchety grubs,[1] beetles, and caterpillars cried: "*Kkkt! Kkkt!* Why do you wake us?" But when the crawling creatures opened their eyes and saw the beauty of Sun Mother, they followed her out of the dark cave onto the earth. Insects

Again a voice called to her. "My daughter, it is time for you to go to the dark caves to wake the sleeping animal spirits."

of every color and shape appeared, and the earth became more beautiful.

As Sun Mother entered the next cave, ice melted under her feet, forming a stream. Her warmth woke the lizards, frogs, and snakes. "*Sssssssst!* Go away!" they hissed. But when they saw beautiful Sun Mother, they followed her, and a stream filled with fish flowed after her.

Accompanied by the crawling and moving creatures, Sun Mother walked to the coldest, darkest cave. Along the ledges of the dark cave were sleeping birds and animals of every kind.

"*HOOOOO!*" the cave owl hooted, and the caterpillars and beetles quaked in terror. The large animals laughed and followed Sun Mother out of the cave.

Sun Mother lay down under a large rivergum tree and rested. All the animals gathered near her. The wind stirred the leaves. All the creatures were content with the gift of life they had received.

---

1. **witchety grubs:** a type of insect larva, the stage between egg and insect.

After resting, Sun Mother spoke to the crawling, moving, feathery, furry creatures and said, "My children, I woke you as a seed is woken in the spring. Now my work is done and I can return to my home in the sky. Treat the earth with care, for it is the earth who has guarded and will guard your sleeping spirits."

Swift as a shooting star, Sun Mother soared up into the western sky. The animals watched in fear. Where was she going? "Come back!" they called. "Sun Mother—" The earth became darker and darker. After a time, it was completely dark. The wind did not whisper. No animal stirred. No fish swam. Everything was still.

Then a little frog croaked loudly. From the corner of her big eye, the frog saw light. Sun Mother was returning in the eastern sky. "Welcome, welcome, Sun Mother!" the animals cried joyously. But Sun Mother did not return to earth. She glided westward across the sky and disappeared.

Again, there was darkness. But the animals were not as frightened as they were before. They understood that Sun Mother had returned to her home in the sky, but each day she would visit them on earth.

But as time passed, the animals forgot the moment when they first received the gift of life. They looked at each other,

The Original Australians

The name *Aborigine* is not the term chosen by the Aborigines for themselves. Instead, it was the name given to native Australians by the European settlers who came to Australia. When the settlers arrived in Australia, there were about five hundred tribes of Aborigines, each with their own language. The meaning of the name is a good fit, however. It comes from the Latin phrase *ab origine,* which literally means "from the beginning"—an echo of the Aborigines' beliefs about their deep connection to the powerful sources of creation.

and they wanted what they did not have. Emu[2] wanted longer legs. Owl wanted larger eyes. Wombat[3] wanted stronger claws. They insulted each other. They mimicked each other. They quarreled so loudly that their cries reached the home of Sun Mother.

Swift as a shooting star, Sun Mother sped to the earth. She gathered everyone together and said, "My children, I love each of you. I wish you to be happy. If you are unhappy with the form you have been given, you will have a chance to choose another one. Consider very carefully now, for the form you choose will be yours for a long time."

Emu grew longer legs so she could run faster than any other bird. Kangaroo grew a pouch so she could keep her babies close to her. Wombat grew stronger claws so he could dig tunnels under the earth. Platypus[4] could not decide what she wanted or where she wanted to live. So she chose everything: a beak, fur, webbed feet, and a tail! Then she moved to a land of flowing waters.

Sun Mother was so amazed watching the animals change shape. She too wanted something new. That night she gave birth to Moon and Morning Star.

A third time Sun Mother spoke to all the creatures and said, "Now when I leave you in the evening, my daughter Moon and my son Morning Star will be with you to give you light."

Moon and Morning Star grew brighter. Moon became big, beautiful, and ready. Some time after Morning Star crossed her path, Moon gave birth to the first woman and the first man.

---

2. **emu** (ē'myo͞o'): large Australian bird that is unable to fly.

3. **wombat** (wäm'bat'): small, bearlike Australian animal that has a pouch and burrows in the ground.

4. **platypus** (plat'ə•pəs): small Australian animal that lives in the water and on land and has webbed feet, a flat tail like a beaver, and a beak like a duck.

"Welcome, welcome, little ones," Sun Mother said to the first woman and the first man. "All around you are your relations—the crawling, moving, feathery, and furry creatures—the water, the grass, the hills, and the wind. This is their place. Now it is your place, too. The place you were born will be called your Dreaming. The place your children will be born will be called their Dreaming.

"Begin your travels. Care for the place of your Dreaming and for all the land for your grandmothers and grandfathers, as well as for your grandchildren. I traveled every step of the earth and it is alive. As I visit the earth each morning, so you too must travel the earth to keep it alive."

With these words, Sun Mother soared up into the sky.

Each morning Sun Mother travels the earth. She brings light to her children, continuing to keep the promise she made at creation.

Not Your Average Rock

Previously known as Ayers Rock, the Aborigines call this giant monolith (literally, "single stone") *Uluru,* meaning "great pebble." However, this "pebble" measures 1,100 feet high and is over two miles long and a mile-and-a-half wide! Perhaps the largest monolith in the world, Uluru is famous for its shifting colors, which change as the sun moves across the sky. It is particularly beautiful at sunset, when the rock glows red-orange. Each day it draws hundreds of admiring tourists. However, to local Aborigines, Uluru is a sacred site. They believe that Uluru is a physical reminder of the deeds performed by the ancestral beings who created the world. Ancient paintings and carvings in the rock's caves are said to tell the Dreamtime stories of these ancestors.

Have you ever longed for the bright warmth of summer during the dark chill of winter? If so, you have something in common with the ancient Greek goddess Demeter (di•mēt'ər). Read on to learn the story of how this earth mother and her daughter, Persephone (pər•sef'ə•nē), first sowed the seeds of the seasons we enjoy today.

Demeter

JOAN D. VINGE

Demeter, the goddess of grains and fruits, was also the goddess of the beautiful flowers and trees that made the world a pleasant place to live in. Demeter loved her daughter, Persephone, so much that she was truly happy only when Persephone was with her.

One day Hades made one of his rare visits to the surface of the earth, driving a black chariot drawn by four coal-black horses. In a meadow he saw Persephone. She was gathering flowers with her friends, and she looked as lovely as the spring day. Hades thought of how her shining beauty would brighten his cold, dark palace. He wanted her for his wife, but he knew that she would never marry him. No one wanted to be the queen of the dead. Besides, he knew her mother would never approve.

But he wanted her for his bride more than he had ever wanted anything. So he charged across the meadow in his black chariot. Persephone looked up

You Need to Know...

Hades (hā'dēz'), brother of Zeus, was the Greek god of the underworld. After Zeus and his two brothers, Hades and Poseidon (pō•sī'dən), defeated the Titans, they agreed that Zeus would be the ruler of all Olympians. When the brothers drew lots to see who would watch over the different parts of the universe, Zeus was assigned to the realm of the air; Poseidon to the sea; and Hades to the underworld.

Olympus was the home of the twelve supreme gods, who were known as the Olympians. Very early on, Olympus was thought to be an actual mountaintop—probably the same mountain that today bears the name Mount Olympus, located in northeastern Greece. However, over time Olympus was understood to be a mystical region unreachable by human beings.

in surprise. She saw a dark stranger bearing down on her; his face was both lordly and terrifying. He put an arm around her and swept her away. A great crack opened in the earth, and he carried her down with him into its depths.

The hills and valleys echoed her cry as the ground closed over her. Demeter, who was never far from her daughter, heard Persephone's cry. She flew like a bird over land and sea, searching for her daughter, but no one knew what had become of her. So Demeter asked the sun. "You look down on all the world," she said. "Tell me what happened to my daughter." Helios, the sun god, told her that Persephone was with Hades, in the land of the dead.

Demeter rushed back to Olympus and demanded that Zeus make Hades give back

Helios, the sun god, told her that Persephone was with Hades, in the land of the dead.

her daughter. Zeus, who wanted his grim brother to be happy for once, said he could not help her. Angry and filled with grief, Demeter left Olympus. She wandered the earth alone. Anyone who saw her saw only a bent, forlorn old woman. She had no heart for her duties as the goddess of growing things or for answering anyone's prayers. The earth suffered along with her. Grasses, flowers, and trees died. Humans and animals starved, for there was nothing to eat. The winter in Demeter's heart had spread over the entire world.

At last the other gods of Olympus realized that something had to be done. Reluctantly Zeus sent Hermes[1] to tell Hades he must give up Persephone. When she heard the news, Persephone smiled for the first time since she had come into that terrible place. She missed the bright and beautiful world—and her mother—terribly.

Hades, on the other hand, was angry and dismayed. Though Persephone had been filled with sadness while she sat at his side, she still seemed to brighten his gloomy world like the sun.

"You are free to go back to your mother," Hermes said to Persephone, "unless you have eaten anything here."

Persephone turned pale, for if you ate the food of the land of death, it meant that you had accepted your fate and were doomed to stay there forever. Persephone had refused to eat the whole time she was in Tartarus[2] or to drink the waters of the spring of Lethe,[3] which brought forgetfulness

---

1. **Hermes** (hur'mēz'): Greek god who acts as a messenger for gods. He is also a guide for travelers.
2. **Tartarus** (tär'tə·rəs): the underworld.
3. **Lethe** (lē'thē): river of forgetfulness that runs through Hades.

United They Stand

In the oldest of the Greek myths, before Zeus and the Olympians make an appearance, Gaia, the earth goddess, reigns supreme over all. The goddesses Demeter, Persephone, and Hecate were actually thought to be three different aspects of this single goddess. Each ruled over a different part of the universe. Hecate, the moon goddess, wandered the sky; Demeter roamed the earth; and Persephone dwelled in the underworld. In some versions of the Demeter myth, it is Hecate—not the sun god Helios—who sees where Persephone has gone. The unity of these three goddesses helps to explain why Demeter and Persephone are so strongly bound together—and why, when they are separated, Demeter loses her power.

Serious About Cereal

In Roman mythology, Demeter was known as Ceres. Like Demeter, Ceres was the goddess of agriculture, fertility, good harvests—and grain. In fact, our word *cereal* comes from the Latin word *cerealis,* meaning "of Ceres." Long ago, the word *cereal* referred only to the actual grasses and grains people grew for food, such as wheat, corn, and oats. Today, these grains are prepared, packaged, and sold as breakfast cereals. The next time you enjoy a bowl of your favorite flakes, you might want to raise a glass of milk to this Greco-Roman deity.

to the spirits of the dead. But once, because she was desperately hungry, she had eaten four small seeds from a pomegranate. Hades knew this.

"She has eaten!" Hades said. "She must stay with me."

"It was only four seeds!" Persephone cried.

Hermes took them both back to Olympus, to the council hall. Persephone ran to her mother. Demeter threatened that she would never bring life back to the world if her daughter was taken from her again. At last Zeus proposed a compromise. Persephone could stay with her mother, in the land of the living, for most of the year. But for four months, one for each pomegranate seed, she had to rejoin Hades in the underworld.

Demeter, Persephone, and Hades all agreed. Demeter then brought spring to the world, turning it green and fruitful, so that everyone could celebrate her daughter's return. Ever since, for eight

months of the year, the world has stayed green and bountiful while Persephone walks upon it. But when the time comes for her to return to the land of death, the world dies, too. It turns bleak and cold, only to be reborn each spring at her return.

Symbols from Nature

- In some versions of this myth, Persephone is said to be gathering violets and lilies when Hades carries her off to the underworld. The lily is widely known in Western culture as a symbol of purity and innocence; likewise, the violet is sometimes considered a symbol of faithfulness.
- The pomegranate's beautiful red-orange color declares it to be a symbol of sun and life. Its seeds are thought to symbolize fruitfulness. In ancient Rome, new brides wore pomegranate wreaths.

We may know more about space than people of long ago did, but we continue to look to the stars for our language and our stories. And, as this Korean folk tale shows, our ancestors shared our space-age desire to explore the heavens—and embrace them.

The Herdsman and the Weaver

TRADITIONAL KOREAN

Once upon a time there lived a king who reigned over the heavens. He had a lovely daughter that knew how to weave the most beautiful cloth in the world. The king would jokingly call the princess "my weaver."

The princess' loom would rattle and knock all day long as the shuttle danced in and out among the threads. Seated there she would make them into cloth that would be the envy of any young woman. She spent her childhood there in front of that loom, until it came time for her to marry.

The king searched his kingdom far and wide to find a suitor for his daughter. One day he met a young man whom he liked very much. "This young man will make a fine husband for my daughter," the king told himself. The young man was a herdsman. He had loved cattle

You Need to Know...

The peninsula of Korea juts off the northeastern coast of China; it also lies within one hundred miles of Japan. Perhaps because of its nearness to these countries, Korea seems to share much of its history and culture with them. The myth of the herdsman and the weaver, for example, is common to all three countries. In China, the day of the lovers' reunion—the seventh day of the seventh month, or July 7—is celebrated as Valentine's Day. In Japan, a summer festival known as Tanabata takes place on this day.

Many ancient cultures told stories about the stars and the gods who dwelt among them. Several of these cultures, such as the Chinese, the Babylonians, and the Egyptians, studied and gathered information about heavenly bodies. By the 1300s B.C., the Chinese had charted the positions of many heavenly bodies and had recorded both solar and lunar eclipses.

ever since he was a little child, so he was very happy in his work.

One beautiful spring day when all of the flowers were in bloom and the birds were singing, the weaver married the herdsman. All the king's subjects were overjoyed at the news.

After the wedding, the young couple spent all their time frolicking about the fields together.

The herdsman deserted his cows. Eventually the cows wandered into the royal garden, trampled all over the royal flowerbed, and ruined it. The weaver no longer wove any beautiful cloth. A thick layer of gray dust gathered on her loom.

When the king saw what was happening, he became very worried. He called the two lovers to him and said, "Son, you are still a herdsman. You must take better care of your cows!" Then he looked at his daughter and said, "You must not abandon your loom."

But the herdsman and the weaver had been married at a very young age, and were still really just children. They

What a Trip!

From Earth, the Milky Way looks like a smear of stars in a distant part of the universe. Actually, our own solar system lies within this monstrous galaxy. A giant spinning pinwheel with five arms, the Milky Way galaxy measures 80,000 to 120,000 light-years across. It contains about 200 billion stars, most of which we cannot see from Earth. Because our solar system is located on the outer edge of one of the arms—the Orion arm—it takes us much longer to orbit the central hub than it would from closer in. At a rate of about 155 miles a second, it takes our solar system between 200 and 250 million years to make one full trip around the block!

didn't realize the importance of what the king was saying to them. They kept roaming in the fields and merrily playing games with each other.

The king became very angry this time. He scolded them at the top of his lungs. "How can you feed yourselves if you don't do any work? You have not obeyed me. I have no choice but to punish you." Pointing at his new son-in-law he said, "From now on, the herdsman must live in the Eastern sky," Then he turned to his daughter, "and the weaver must live in the Western sky."

When the herdsman and the weaver heard this, they both cried, "Oh, Father, please forgive us. We know we were wrong to play in the fields all day. We promise to do our share of work. Please let us stay together. We love each other more than anything!"

But the king was not moved by their tears. The herdsman and the weaver were forced to part. He went East and she went West.

They were so sad that eventually the king began to feel sorry for them. Finally he decided to let them meet once a year on the banks of the Milky Way River. All year long, the two lovers counted the days and nights while thinking of each other. Both now knew that they had been disobedient to their father and king.

▲ *The Moon of the Milky Way* by Tsukioka Yoshitoshi.

The day finally came when they were allowed to have their yearly meeting. With high hopes, each headed for their meeting place by Milky Way River. But when they reached it, the river had become so wide and the night so dark that they could not see each other.

The herdsman and the weaver stood on the banks of the Milky Way River and cried. Tears rolled down their cheeks and into the river. The water from their tears flowed down the river and then became rain. The rain then fell to the earth until the ground was all wet and soggy. The seas rose higher and higher.

The herdsman and the weaver stood on the banks of the Milky Way River and cried. Their tears flowed down the river and then became rain.

The fields and gardens of the kingdom were flooded. Not only that, the homes of the king's subjects were swept away in the waves.

The animals of the kingdom became very alarmed indeed. They all met to decide what to do. Each animal took turns telling everyone at the meeting what they thought would be a good way to stop the flood of tears. Some made low grunts and some made high squeaks. Some of them whistled when they talked.

Finally one animal came up with a suggestion. "We must help the herdsman and the weaver get together again. Otherwise this rain will never stop."

"Yes," said another, "let's build a bridge for them!"

"That's it!" exclaimed another animal. "We must build a great bridge!" All of the animals agreed. But none of them knew how to go about building a bridge. Animals don't usually know how to build bridges. They all lay around looking at one another, twisting their tails in silence.

Finally some crows and magpies chirped up to the group. "Let us birds do it," said one. "We can fly to the Milky Way River," said another. "And make ourselves into a bridge."

So all of the crows in the world got together and made a big flock with their cousins, the magpies, and flew up to the Milky Way River. They flew tightly together holding on to each other with their talons. Soon they stretched from one bank of the river to the other.

The herdsman and the weaver were very surprised to see a bridge of birds. "What is this?" they exclaimed. "Now we can cross the Milky Way River and be together again!"

The herdsman and the weaver ran across the backs of the birds. In the middle of the bridge of birds they met holding each other in tight embrace.

Right around this time the heavy rains slowed to a drizzle. But then the two lovers had to return to their homes in the East and the West for yet another lonely year.

Wish upon a Star

In Japan, this folk tale merged with Japanese legends about a heavenly weaver known as Tanabatatsume. For centuries, the day of the lovers' reunion has been celebrated in Japan as Tanabata. The festival originally focused on the art of weaving, but today it signals the coming of summer. To celebrate, many people decorate bamboo branches with narrow strips of paper, which symbolize the weaver's colorful threads. On each strip is written a poem, a proverb, or a wish for the coming year. Like summer Christmas trees, the cheerful branches are placed in gardens, children's bedrooms, and schools. After the festival, they are set afloat on rivers. It is hoped that the branches carry away with them any lingering traces of bad luck.

After that, on the seventh day of the seventh moon of every year, all of the crows and magpies would fly to the Milky Way River to form a bridge. The herdsman and the weaver would meet on that special day of every year by crossing the river on the backs of the kind flock of birds.

Crows and magpies have not always lost their feathers once a year. But ever since they started forming flocks to fly to the Milky Way River, ever since they started helping the herdsman and the princess see each other, they have lost their feathers after the seventh day of the seventh moon. Now you know why everyone in the kingdom treats them kindly.

It Is Better To Die Forever

RETOLD BY CHEWING BLACKBONES

Long, long ago, there were only two persons in the world: Old Man and Old Woman. One time when they were traveling about the earth, Old Woman said to Old Man, "Now let us come to an agreement of some kind. Let us decide how the people shall live when they shall be on the earth."

"Well," replied Old Man, "I am to have the first say in everything."

"I agree with you," said the Old Woman. "That is—if I may have the second say."

Then Old Man began his plans. "The women will have the duty of tanning the hides. They will rub animals' brains on the hides to make them soft and scrape them with scraping tools. All this they will do very quickly, for it will not be hard work."

"No," said Old Woman, "I will not agree to this. They must tan hides in the way you say; but it must be very hard work, so that the good workers may be found out."

"Well," said Old Man, "we will let the people have eyes and mouths, straight up and down in their faces."

> ### You Need to Know...
> The character called Old Man appears in many Blackfeet legends. Also known as Napi, Old Man is thought to be the offspring of the Sun and the Moon. He is honored as the maker of mountains, rivers, forests, animals, and people themselves, including Old Woman. He is also known to be a trickster and, occasionally, a danger to the creatures he made—especially those he considers a nuisance. It is said that after Old Man taught the Blackfeet how to live, he went away. However, first he made a promise. "I will always take care of you," he said, "and some day, I will come back."

"No," replied Old Woman, "let us not have them that way. We will have the eyes and mouths in the faces, as you say, but they shall be set crosswise."

"Well," said Old Man, "the people shall have ten fingers on each hand."

"Oh, no!" replied Old Woman. "That will be too many. They will be in the way. There will be four fingers and one thumb on each hand."

So the two went on until they had provided for everything in the lives of the people who were to be.

"What shall we do about life and death?" asked Old Woman. "Should the people live forever, or should they die?"

Old Woman and Old Man had difficulty agreeing about this. Finally Old Man said, "I will tell you what we will do. I will throw a buffalo chip into the water. If it floats, the people will die for four days and then come to life again; if it sinks, they will die forever."

Sole Survivors

The Blackfeet call themselves Siksikawa (shēk•shēk•ä•wä), which literally means "black foot." The name refers to the tribe's wearing of trademark black moccasins, a custom with mysterious origins. Some Blackfeet say that their ancestors painted the moccasins' soles black. Others tell of brave forebears who walked near prairie fires. Either way, the Blackfeet are survivors. The Blackfeet probably migrated west from the Great Lakes region during the 1600s. They lived on the Northern Plains until white settlers began pushing westward. Like other Indian tribes, the Blackfeet suffered as the white hunters preyed upon the buffalo. However, the Blackfeet held fast to their beliefs and traditions. Today, they are one of the tribes in the northwest. Their reservations are located in Montana and in Alberta, Canada.

▲ *A Blackfoot Indian on Horse-Back* after a painting by Karl Bodmer.

So he threw a buffalo chip into the water, and it floated.

Then Old Woman threw the rock into the water, and it sank to the bottom.

"There," said she. "It is better for the people to die forever. If they did not, they would not feel sorry for each other, and there would be no sympathy in the world."

"Well," said Old Man, "let it be that way."

After a time, Old Woman had a daughter, who soon became sick and died. The mother was very sorry then that they had agreed that people should die forever. "Let us have our say over again," she said.

"No," replied Old Man. "Let us not change what we have agreed upon."

And so people have died ever since.

In this story from India, the Buddha uses the mustard seed to teach a lesson. Stories that teach are common to many cultures and religions and are usually about an ordinary event. However, there is always a greater lesson to be learned. What lesson does the story of the mustard seed teach?

The Mustard Seed

T. W. Rhys Davids

Kisagotami is the name of a young girl, whose marriage with the only son of a wealthy man was brought about in true fairy-tale fashion. She had one child, but when the beautiful boy could run alone, it died. The young girl, in her love for it, carried the dead child clasped to her bosom, and went from house to house of her pitying friends asking them to give her medicine for it.

But a Buddhist mendicant[1], thinking "She does not understand," said to her, "My good girl, I myself have no such medicine as you ask for, but I think I know of one who has."

"O tell me who that is," said Kisagotami.

"The Buddha can give you medicine. Go to him," was the answer.

She went to Gautama, and doing homage to him said, "Lord and master, do you know any medicine that will be good for my child?"

"Yes, I know of some," said the teacher.

Now it was the custom for patients or their friends to provide the herbs which the doctors required, so she asked what herbs he would want.

"I want some mustard seed," he said; and when the

---

1. **mendicant** (men′di•kənt): beggar.

poor girl eagerly promised to bring some of so common a drug, he added, "You must get it from some house where no son, or husband, or parent, or slave has died."

"Very good," she said, and went to ask for it, still carrying her dead child with her.

The people said, "Here is mustard seed, take it."

But when she asked, "In my friend's house has any son died, or husband, or a parent or slave?" they answered, "Lady, what is this that you say? The living are few, but the dead are many."

Then she went to other houses, but one said, "I have lost a son"; another, "We have lost our parents"; another, "I have lost my slave."

At last, not being able to find a single house where no one had died, her mind began to clear, and summoning up resolution, she left the dead body of her child in a forest, and returning to the Buddha paid him homage.

He said to her, "Have you the mustard seed?"

"My lord," she replied, "I have not. The people tell me that the living are few, but the dead are many."

▲ A wall painting of Buddha and his followers.

Sometimes what looks like an ending is really a beginning. Can you find any seeds of hope buried in the dark tangle of this ancient Norse myth?

The End of the World

STEVE ZEITLIN

One night, Odin's son Balder, fairest of all divine beings, had a frightening dream about his own death. He told his father, who convened a council of the gods. Fearing danger, the council sent the Goddess Frigg to extract an oath from every man, woman, and child, every plant, every thing made of metal, wood, and stone. All had to promise that they would do no harm to Balder.

Balder, told that the world's creatures had promised not to harm him, invited the gods in the halls of Asgard[1] to throw stones and darts at him. They all laughed as the missiles fell harmlessly from his body and bounced against the marble floors.

But the wicked Loki grew ever more angry. He took on the disguise of a woman and talked with Frigg. He learned that one little plant, the mistletoe, had not taken the oath. Frigg had thought it too young to threaten Balder. Filled with spite, Loki pulled up the little mistletoe and persuaded Hoder, the blind god,

---

You Need to Know...

Norse mythology is not as hopeful as the mythologies of other cultures. In fact, it's downright gloomy. The Norse gods fully expected disaster and death to befall them and Asgard, their home. The final destruction of the world, or Ragnarok (rag'nə•räk'), was believed to be constantly at hand. It was inevitable that the gods would be forced to meet their enemies and suffer defeat. The world of the gods would be no more. However, even though death itself was certain, one's approach to death was not. One could choose to die heroically, spurning the enemy even in defeat. Or one could be a coward and flee. To the ancient Norse people, dying a heroic death was the ultimate good—the only true measure of success in their dismal world.

---

1. **Asgard** (äs'gärd'): home of the Norse gods.

to hurl it at Balder, guiding his hand as he threw. The mistletoe pierced Balder like a dart, and he fell dead to the earth.

Bitter tears fell from the eyes of the gods, and Odin's were the most bitter of all. He asked for a warrior to ride to the kingdom of Hel and attempt to bring Balder back from the dead. Borrowing Odin's horse Sleipnir, the god Hermod[2] rode down the dark road to that dim land, over the fiery bridge that spanned the Resounding River. A maiden guarding this bridge came out in wonder to see who approached with such noise and tumult. Balder, she said, had already passed that way, guarded by five troops of dead warriors. But he was not like the other dead men; he still had the rose-colored cheeks of the living.

At last Hermod reached the Hel gate, and Sleipnir leaped over it with ease. Balder was seated on the platform reserved for new arrivals. Hel was willing to release him on the condition that all things in the world, living or dead, would weep for him. But should any creature refuse to weep, she said, then Balder must stay with her and never return to Asgard. Hermod bid Balder farewell, and he and Sleipnir headed home.

▲ Odin seated on his throne, attended by his dogs and ravens.

At the request of the gods, all things—men and beasts— did indeed weep for Balder. Even stones and metals became moist with tears. But as the messenger of the gods traveled

---

2. **Hermod:** one of Frigga's sons.

to the far reaches of the kingdom, he came upon a Giantess,[3] alone in a cave. When he asked her to weep for Balder, she offered a horrible reply:

Alive or dead, the old man's son
has been no use to me.
Let Hel hold what she has!

The Giantess was none other than Loki himself, seeking in his malice to keep the fair Balder in Hel!

With Loki's wickedness unleashed in the universe, the ties of kinship and the rules of law collapsed. Evil ran rampant. The Giants crossed the sea in a boat made of dead men's fingernails, with Loki as the steersman. They crossed the bridge of fire, tearing it asunder with their weight. The vicious wolf Fenris[4] held the sun and moon and the space

---

3. **Giantess:** along with the Giants, enemy of the Norse gods.

4. **Fenris** (fen'ris): chained wolf eager to devour Odin. The sun and moon are chased across the sky by wolves.

Who's Who?

Here is a quick look at some of the key players in this dark Norse drama:

- Odin is the sky-father and ruler of all the gods. His job is to postpone the day of doom for as long as possible. In another Norse myth on page 97, you will read how Odin goes in search of new wisdom and suffers in exchange for it.
- Frigg, Odin's wife, is known for her wisdom, silence, and secretiveness. This goddess is often shown spinning golden threads at her spinning wheel. What she is weaving, of course, always remains a mystery.
- Loki (lō'kē), a trickster and fire god, is the master of cunning and the son of a Giant. The Giants are the ever-present enemies of the gods and are part of their downfall. These powerful creatures win the small battles of everyday life, and they are also guaranteed total victory at the end of the world.

between earth and heaven between his deadly jaws. The World Serpent[5] emerged from the deep, foam spewing from the corners of his mouth.

When the fiends neared the Rainbow Bridge, the sound of Heimdall's[6] horn and the crowing of the cock on the World Tree heralded the approach of the enemy. When the signal came, Odin led his army out onto the field where the last battle was destined to be fought. Fire flashed from the eyes and nostrils of the wolf Fenris as he devoured the sun. The mighty serpent vomited great torrents of venom upon the waters. The stars flew from their places, and the heavens cracked open.

Odin's sharp blade tore into Fenris; his horse Sleipnir, up on his hind legs, clawed at the wolf. Valiantly they struggled, but the savage Fenris devoured them both. Odin's young son Vidar avenged his father, tearing the monster's jaws apart.

Wearing his belt of power, Thor[7] swung the hammer Mjollnir,

---

5. **World Serpent:** is wound around the earth at the bottom of the ocean.

6. **Heimdall** (hām'däl'): keeper of the rainbow bridge that leads to Asgard.

7. **Thor** (thôr): Norse god of thunder, the strongest of the gods.

flattening the great serpent. Dying, the serpent bit him, and the mighty Thor crumpled, slowly twisted to the ground, and died from the poison. Heimdall and Loki slew each other. The sky fell, and the stars vanished. Fire and smoke rose high, and the rising sea engulfed the world.

But this was not the end, for the World Tree survived untouched. During the terrible winter struggle, the sons of the gods, along with a single man and woman, sheltered within its bark. When the devastating battles ended, they came out into the bright light to begin their lives anew. Once more an eagle was seen in the sky, and a new sun moved across the heavens. As they rested on the fresh grass of the cleansed world, the young gods found the golden playing pieces for the games that Odin and Thor once enjoyed in Asgard.

Mistletoe Mystery

Mistletoe can grow on trees by sending roots into tree trunks. To some ancient people, it seemed mysterious that the plant could grow without roots in the ground. Mistletoe was therefore thought to be a gift from the gods. Here are some other mistletoe beliefs and traditions from days gone by.

- When ancient Druid enemies met under mistletoe, it is said that they laid down their weapons and rested peacefully until morning.
- Early European farmers believed that mistletoe kept milk from souring and made butter easier to churn. They hung mistletoe boughs near the cows in their barns.
- The ancient Celts hung mistletoe over their babies' cradles. This was said to keep the babies from being kidnapped by fairies.

CHAPTER 2
The Deeds of Gods and Heroes

Heroes Old and New

The heroes in this chapter have much in common with modern heroes.

Luke Skywalker of the first *Star Wars* trilogy is trained by mentor Obi-Wan Kenobi before leading a rebellion against the evil Darth Vader—and his success is made possible by help from his friends. Bellerophon (page 47) is also helped by a mentor and other loyal friends.

Peter Parker, bitten by a mutant spider, now possesses superhuman qualities. As Spider-Man, he uses these powers—including web casting and surface clinging—to fight crime and save innocents from the hand of evil. Like Spider-Man, the early Anglo-Saxon hero Beowulf (page 78) single-handedly overcomes powerful foes.

Superman of comic-book and movie fame was one of the first comic-book superheroes to be created. Disguised as the mild-mannered Clark Kent, Superman comes to the rescue whenever needed, often aided by Lois Lane, a fellow reporter on the *Daily Planet* who later becomes

SPIDER-MAN: ™&©2002 Marvel Characters, Inc. Used with permission.

INVESTIGATE: What other modern heroes can you identify?

▲ A representation of the statue of Zeus at Olympia.

his wife. See how the super-human Rama comes to the rescue of his wife, Sita (page 72).

Heroic Heights

Gods and heroes weren't the only wonders of the ancient world. While humans were creating mythical heroes in the realm of the imagination and worshiping a multitude of gods, they were also creating marvelous objects in the actual world. Known as the Seven Wonders of the Ancient World, these structures have long been admired for their massive size and clever construction.

However, for the people who built them, they were more than just glory-seeking experiments. Many of the structures had important practical or sacred purposes, too. As tombs, temples, or religious icons, they helped humans avoid the perils of this world—and the next. By building temples in honor of the gods, humans hoped to secure their favor and protection. An example of this was the giant statue of Zeus at Olympia, much admired by people who attended the early Olympic games. We, too, benefit from our ancestors' efforts. Like larger-than-life heroes themselves, the Seven Wonders fill us with awe, spark our imaginations, and inspire us to push onward and upward in our own lives—step by step and brick by brick.

Is a hero someone who has more good luck than others—or someone who stares bad luck in the face? Read this Greco-Roman myth to discover one answer to this question.

Bellerophon

REX WARNER

Bellerophon[1] was son of the King of Corinth[2] and grew up to be a young man of remarkable strength and beauty, brave also, and ready to undertake any difficult adventure.

Soon after he grew to manhood he unluckily and by accident killed one of his relations and, to avoid the guilt of blood, he left his native land and went to live in Argos.[3]

Here Proetus was king and here Bellerophon received a generous welcome. The king admired the young man's courage and beauty; he was glad to have his services in peace and war, and raised him to a position of honor in his court. Bellerophon might have lived for long in Argos, had it not been that the king's wife Antea fell in love with him.

> **You Need to Know...**
> Unlike modern-day Greece, ancient Greece was not a unified nation. Instead, it was a collection of city-states, each consisting of a city or a town, all of the nearby villages, and the surrounding countryside. Most city-states were either democracies or ruled by a few wealthy men, and each had its own laws. The city-states were fiercely independent and often got into arguments with each other. Still, a common language, religion, and culture held these mini-kingdoms together. One element of this shared culture was a code of hospitality. It dictated that guests were to be given the royal treatment: a warm welcome, a meal or feast, and often lavish gifts. To break this code was to invite the wrath of Zeus himself. However, as you will see in this story, hospitality was not always practical—especially if you were one king trying to avoid a feud with another. The ancient Greeks, though, were logical, creative thinkers. As you read, look for characters whose problem-solving skills are—in a word—heroic.

---

1. **Bellerophon** (bə•ler'ə•fän')
2. **Corinth** (kôr'inth): ancient Greek city.
3. **Argos** (är'gäs): an ancient city-state in Greece.

She approached him with endearing words, begging him to take her from her husband. Bellerophon, grateful to the king for his hospitality and for his many kindnesses, indignantly refused to listen to the shameful suggestions of Antea. Then her love turned to hatred. She went to Proetus and said: "If you have any respect for your wife, I demand that this young man be put to death. He is on fire with love for me, and has already attempted by force to take me away from you."

Proetus believed the false words of his wife, but still he did not wish himself to have the guilt and unpopularity of putting the young man to death. He therefore sent him to visit his father-in-law Iobates, King of Lycia[4] in Asia Minor,[5] and before he left he gave him a sealed message in which was written: "If you love me and value my friendship, ask no questions but immediately put the bearer of this message to death."

Bellerophon took the message with no suspicion that he was carrying his own death-warrant, and set out on his voyage across the sea to Lycia. When he arrived, King Iobates, knowing him to be the favorite of the King of Argos, welcomed him warmly and feasted him in the rich halls of

▲ Winged Pegasus flies among the stars

_____

4. **Lycia** (lish′ə)

5. **Asia Minor:** large peninsula between the Black Sea and the Mediterranean Sea.

his palace. They were merry and friendly together at the feast, but when it was over Bellerophon gave the King the message which he had brought, and the King read it in sorrow and amazement, unwilling to believe that so gallant a young man could have injured his protector, unwilling too to offend against the sacred laws of hospitality by killing a stranger whom he had entertained in his own halls. Nevertheless he could not refuse to obey the clear instructions of the King of Argos. A plan occurred to him by which it seemed certain that the young man would meet his death, while the king himself would not incur the guilt of having directly brought it about. Bellerophon had already offered to help the king in any way in which his services could be used. Now the king ordered him to find and to destroy the Chimera,[6] an invincible monster that lived in rocky caves

---

6. **Chimera** (kĭ·mir'ə)

Rising Above It All

Medusa was the most famous of the Gorgons (gôr'gənz), a family of hideous monsters who were part bird and part woman. In addition to their frightening wings and claws, the Gorgons each sported a headful of writhing snakes. Indeed, the Gorgons were so horrible to behold that those who did so were instantly turned to stone. However, good can sometimes spring up out of evil. When Medusa was slain by the hero Perseus, the winged steed Pegasus was said to have risen out of her dead body. This strange birth seems to have doomed poor Pegasus to encounters with a string of unseemly creatures. In addition to his close encounter with the Chimera, Pegasus also helped to slay a frightful sea monster known as Cetus. As a reward, Pegasus was placed in the sky as a constellation, where he still shines today.

and ravaged all the country around. The Chimera had a lion's head, the body of a great shaggy she-goat, and a dragon's tail. Out of its mouth it breathed such blasts of fire and smoke that no one could approach it. It moved with incredible speed, hunting down men and cattle, so that for miles around its rocky lair the country was a wilderness.

Bellerophon knew the difficulties and dangers of his task, but he gladly and willingly undertook it. His courage, however, would not have proved enough if he had not been helped by the goddess Minerva.[7] She told him that he could never conquer the Chimera without the help of Pegasus,[8] the winged horse who had sprung to life from the blood of Medusa,[9] whom Perseus[10] slew, and who now lived on Mount Helicon with the Muses,[11] never yet having felt the weight of a man upon his back. So Bellerophon set out once more on a long journey. He found the horse, a wonderful and swift animal, snow-white and smooth as silk not only over all his skin but also where the gleaming feathery wings lay along his shoulders. For a whole day Bellerophon tried to throw a bridle round the animal's neck, but Pegasus would never allow him to come close enough to do so. Whenever Bellerophon approached, the horse would either gallop away out of reach or would rise on wings in the air, alighting further off in the cool meadows where he grazed. In the evening, worn out and despairing, Bellerophon lay down to sleep. He dreamed that Minerva had come to him and given him a golden bridle. On waking up he found that this was actually what had happened. At his side was a beautiful bridle of gold and, with this in his hand, he

---

7. **Minerva** (mi•nʉr'və): Roman goddess of wisdom.

8. **Pegasus** (peg'ə•səs)

9. **Medusa** (mə•do͞o'sə): snake-haired Gorgon.

10. **Perseus** (pʉr'sē•əs): Greek hero who was the son of Zeus.

11. **Muses** (myo͞oz'iz): Greek goddesses of literature, the arts, and the sciences.

immediately set out again to look for Pegasus. When the horse saw the bridle, he bowed his head and came gently forward, willingly allowing Bellerophon to bridle and to mount him. Then he sprang into the air and sped like a shooting star through the clouds to the country where the Chimera lived; for the horse was a divine horse, knowing exactly for what reason he was wanted.

Flying over the deep gullies and rocky caves in the mountains, Bellerophon saw beneath him the red glow of fire and smoke ascending into the air. He checked the course of Pegasus and flew nearer to the earth, and soon appeared the vast body of the monster as it came raging out of its lair. Pegasus hovered over it like a hawk hovers above

▲ Bellerophon killing the Chimera.

That's Unreal

If you asked a five-year-old to draw a scary monster, she might come up with something like the Chimera. With a lion's head, a goat's body, and a snake's tail—not to mention a fire-breathing mouth—the Chimera is clearly the product of a *very* active imagination. Today, we use the word *chimera* to refer to any outlandish scheme or idea. And when scientists graft, or transplant, a part of one plant or animal onto another, the resulting organism is also called a *chimera.*

its prey, and first Bellerophon shot his arrows into the great goat-like body below him, until the ground was drenched in blood. Then he swooped down through the clouds of smoke, thrusting his sword over and over again into the animal's neck and flanks. It was not long before the Chimera lay dead and sprawling on the ground. Then Bellerophon cut off its head and said good-bye to the noble horse who had helped him, since Minerva had told him that once his task was accomplished, he must let the animal go. Pegasus was never again mounted by any mortal man. He sped away like lightning. Some say that he went back to the grassy pastures of Helicon and that where his hoof struck the ground there issued forth the fountain of Hippocrene. Others say that it was at this time that Jupiter set the winged horse among the stars.

Bellerophon himself returned to King Iobates carrying with him the head of the Chimera.

Bellerophon himself returned to King Iobates carrying with him the head of the Chimera. The king was glad that the monster had been destroyed and he admired the courage of the young man who had destroyed it. Still he felt bound to carry out the instructions of the King of Argos and secure Bellerophon's death. Next he sent him to fight against the Solymi, a tribe of fierce mountaineers who lived upon the borders of Lycia and who had conquered the king's armies whenever they had been sent against them. Bellerophon, with a small force, marched into, the mountains, killed or made prisoners of the whole tribe, and returned without a wound.

Next he was sent against the warrior nation of the Amazons, the fierce women who had conquered so many armies of men in battle. These also Bellerophon defeated, and now the king determined on a last plan by which he could do the will of the King of Argos. He picked out of his forces the best and strongest of his fighting men, and told them to lay an ambush for Bellerophon as he was on his way back from his conquest of the Amazons. Again the gods preserved him. With his own hand he killed every one of his attackers, and when he reached the king's court Iobates exclaimed: "There can be no doubt that the young man is innocent. Otherwise the gods would not have saved his life so often."

He gave Bellerophon his daughter to be his wife, sharing with him his riches and his throne. And when Iobates died, Bellerophon became King of Lycia.

The hero you are about to meet might have a funny-sounding name, but his powers are far from laughable. Follow this Native American god upstream as he seeks the source of a gigantic problem.

Glooscap Fights the Water Monster

RETOLD BY RICHARD ERDOES AND ALFONSO ORTIZ

Glooscap yet lives, somewhere at the southern edge of the world. He never grows old, and he will last as long as this world lasts. Sometimes Glooscap gets tired of running the world, ruling the animals, regulating nature, instructing people how to live. Then he tells us: "I'm tired of it. Good-bye; I'm going to make myself die now." He paddles off in his magic white canoe and disappears in misty clouds. But he always comes back. He cannot abandon the people forever, and they cannot live without him.

Glooscap is a spirit, a medicine man,[1] a sorcerer. He can make men and women smile. He can do anything.

Glooscap made all the animals, creating them to be peaceful and useful to humans. When he

You Need to Know...

Several groups of American Indians recognize Glooscap as their creator, teacher, and friend.

- The Passamaquoddy people were expert fishers and trappers, navigating the Northeast woodlands in their sleek canoes and living in cone-shaped wigwams. Today, about six hundred Passamaquoddy live on reservations in Maine.
- The Maliseet share the language, history, and customs of the Passamaquoddy people. Before the arrival of Europeans, the Maliseet lived in the borderlands between northern New England and Canada. Members of the Maliseet tribe today reside in both Maine and Canada.
- The Micmac may have been the first Native Americans to encounter Europeans when the Vikings came here in the eleventh century. In the early American colonies, the Micmac were known for their woven baskets. Many modern-day Micmac live in Boston and New York City.

---

1. **medicine man:** someone with supernatural powers over disease and spirits.

formed the first squirrel, it was as big as a whale. "What would you do if I let you loose on the world?" Glooscap asked, and the squirrel attacked a big tree, chewing it to pieces in no time. "You're too destructive for your size," said Glooscap, and remade him small. The first beaver also was as big as a whale, and it built a dam that flooded the country from horizon to horizon. Glooscap said, "You'll drown all the people if I let you loose like this." He tapped the beaver on the back, and it shrank to its present size. The first moose was so tall that it reached to the sky and looked altogether different from the way it looks now. It trampled everything in its path—forests, mountains, everything. "You'll ruin everything," Glooscap said. "You'll step on people and kill them." Glooscap tapped the moose on the back to make it small, but the moose refused to become smaller. So Glooscap killed it and recreated it in a different size and with a different look. In this way Glooscap made everything as it should be.

Glooscap had also created a village and taught the people there everything they needed to know. They were happy hunting and fishing. Men and women were happy in love. Children were happy playing. Parents cherished their children, and children respected their parents. All was well as Glooscap had made it.

The village had one spring, the only source of water far and wide, that always flowed with pure, clear, cold water. But one day the spring ran dry; only a little bit of slimy ooze issued from it. It stayed dry even in the fall when the rains came, and in the spring when the snows melted. The people wondered, "What shall we do? We can't live without water."

The wise men and elders held a council and decided to send a man north to the source of the spring to see why it had run dry.

This man walked a long time until at last he came to a village. The people there were not like humans; they had webbed hands and feet. Here the brook widened out. There was some water in it, not much, but a little, though it was slimy, yellowish, and stinking. The man was thirsty from his walk and asked to be given a little water, even if it was bad.

"We can't give you any water," said the people with the webbed hands and feet, "unless our great chief permits it. He wants all the water for himself."

"Where is your chief?" asked the man.

"You must follow the brook further up," they told him.

The man walked on and at last met the big chief. When he saw him he trembled with fright, because the chief was a monster so huge that if one stood at his feet, one could not see his head. The monster filled the whole valley from end to end. He had dug himself a huge hole and dammed it up, so that all the water was in it and none could flow into the stream bed. And he had fouled the water and made it poisonous, so that stinking mists covered its slimy surface.

The monster had a mile-wide, grinning mouth going from ear to ear. His dull yellow eyes started out of his head like huge pine knots. His body was bloated and covered with warts as big as mountains. The monster stared dully at the man with his protruding eyes and finally said in a fearsome croak: "Little man, what do you want?"

The man was terrified, but he said: "I come from a village far downstream. Our only spring ran dry, because you're keeping all the water for yourself. We would like you to let us have some of this water. Also, please don't muddy it so much."

The monster blinked at him a few times. Finally he croaked:

Do as you please,
Do as you please,

I don't care,
I don't care,

If you want water,
If you want water,

Go elsewhere!

The Wisdom of Animals

In many Native American cultures, animals are thought of as sacred symbols. When an animal is chosen to represent a tribe or an individual, this animal is known as a *totem.* Often, a totem shares certain qualities with the tribe or person it represents. It is also thought to lead those who honor it toward greater wisdom. Here are a few examples:

- As a totem, the moose grants the power of self-esteem. It can help people to see and appreciate the wisdom that exists within them.
- The squirrel is the gatherer and saver. It can teach humans how to save their energy for times when it may be needed.
- The coyote is the trickster, helping us to learn through our mistakes.

The man said, "We need the water. The people are dying of thirst." The monster replied:

I don't care,
I don't care,

Don't bother me,
Don't bother me,

Go away,
Go away,

Or I'll swallow you up!

The monster opened his mouth wide from ear to ear, and inside it the man could see the many things that the creature had killed. The monster gulped a few times and smacked his lips with a noise like thunder. At this the man's courage broke, and he turned and ran away as fast as he could.

Back at his village the man told the people: "Nothing can be done. If we complain, this monster will swallow us up. He'll kill us all."

The people were in despair. "What shall we do?" they cried. Now, Glooscap knows everything that goes on in the world, even before it happens. He sees everything with his inward eye. He said: "I must set things right. I'll have to get water for the people!"

Then Glooscap girded himself for war. He painted his body with paint as red as blood. He made himself twelve feet tall. He used two huge clamshells for his earrings. He put a hundred black eagle feathers and a hundred white eagle feathers in his scalp lock. He painted yellow rings around his eyes. He twisted his mouth into a snarl and made himself look ferocious. He stamped, and the earth trembled. He uttered his fearful war cry, and it echoed and re-echoed from all the mountains. He grasped a huge mountain in his hand, a mountain composed of flint, and from it made himself a single knife sharp as a weasel's teeth. "Now

I am going," he said, striding forth among thunder and lightning, with mighty eagles circling above him. Thus Glooscap came to the village of the people with webbed hands and feet.

"I want water," he told them. Looking at him, they were afraid. They brought him a little muddy water. "I think I'll get more and cleaner water," he said. Glooscap went upstream and confronted the monster. "I want clean water," he said, "a lot of it, for the people downstream."

Ho! Ho!
Ho! Ho!

All the waters are mine!
All the waters are mine!

Go away!
Go away!

Or I'll kill you!

"Slimy lump of mud!" cried Glooscap. "We'll see who will be killed!" They fought. The mountains shook. The earth split open. The swamp smoked and burst into flames. Mighty trees were shivered into splinters.

The monster opened its huge mouth wide to swallow Glooscap. Glooscap made himself taller than the tallest tree, and even the monster's mile-wide mouth was too small for him. Glooscap seized his great flint knife and slit the monster's bloated belly. From the wound gushed a mighty stream, a roaring river, tumbling, rolling, foaming down, down, down, gouging out for itself a vast, deep bed, flowing by the village and on to the great sea of the east.

"That should be enough water for the people," said Glooscap. He grasped the monster and squeezed him in his mighty palm, squeezed and squeezed and threw him away, flinging him into the swamp. Glooscap had squeezed this great creature into a small bullfrog, and ever since, the bullfrog's skin has been wrinkled because Glooscap squeezed so hard.

It's Not Easy Being Green

Frogs adore water. They sit in it, splash in it, swim in it. As amphibians, frogs *need* water to live. This may be why frogs appear as water guardians in Native American lore. When there was plenty of water, it was Frog Woman who was honored. However, during times of drought, Frog Woman was often cast as a water thief or monster. A hero, such as Coyote, had to make her give up the water. Like the giant in this tale, frogs are also ravenous eaters. They feast on anything they can snatch with their sticky tongues— from bugs to snakes. As keepers of water and food, frogs are also honored by Native Americans for their abilities to bestow these necessary gifts and to cleanse, heal, and help things grow.

Are some of your heroes athletes? Read this Mayan story to see how two brothers who were ballplayers became superheroes when they accepted the challenge of their lives.

The Twins and the Ballgame

AMY CRUSE

It would take too long to tell of all the tricks these mischievous twins played during their boyhood and youth. When they were nearly grown to men, they were set one day to clear a piece of ground that was covered with weeds and bushes, and make it ready for the planting of maize. They did not like hard work, so they laid a spell on their tools, which forthwith began to work by themselves.

Away went the twins for a day's hunting, and coming back at night they smeared their faces and hands with soil, and went home to their grandmother, groaning and complaining how tired they were, and boasting of the land they had cleared during the day. The old woman believed them, gave them a good supper, and praised them for their work; but in the morning when she went to look, she found the ground covered with weeds and bushes, just as it had

You Need to Know...

- The Mayan people once lived in what are now Guatemala and southern Mexico. Abundant corn crops gave the Maya enough wealth and free time to study the stars, build pyramids and palaces, and develop a mathematical system. They also created a written language using hieroglyphs. Most Mayan books were destroyed by the conquering Spaniards in the 1500s, but a version of their sacred book, the *Popol Vuh*, survived.
- "The Twins and the Ballgame" is taken from the *Popol Vuh*, which also contains a story about the twins' father and uncle, who were gods. Before the twins were born, these gods accepted a challenge to play ball with the kings of the underworld. Once in Hades, the brothers were imprisoned and killed. However, the twins' father had first managed to marry an underworld princess. She left the underworld to live with her late husband's mother and to give birth to the powerful but mischievous twins.

The Deeds of Gods and Heroes **61**

been before. She came back to the house in a rage, and scolded them loudly for coming to her with a false tale that had induced her to give them food and lodging.

The twins were very much surprised and went out to look for themselves. There in truth was the land they had left so clear and smooth the night before once more choked with weeds. This would never do; and they set to work to find out who it was that had played such a trick upon them. Soon by their magic arts they discovered that the wild animals, not wishing the brothers to spend all their time in hunting, had replaced at night all that the magic tools had cleared away during the day.

Hun-Apu and Xbalanque listened while the rat told them how their father and their uncle had been lured to their death by the lords of Hades.

"*Ha!*" said the twins, "we must see to this." So they got a large net and spread it over the ground. "If the creatures come again tonight," they said, "they will not find it so easy to get away again."

That night the animals stole to the field once more, and found themselves entangled in the folds of the great net. They struggled hard, and all managed to get away except the rat, though the deer and the rabbit left their tails behind, and have suffered from that loss ever since.

In the morning the brothers came to see what had happened. They saw the signs of the struggle, but found no creature on whom they could vent their anger save the poor trembling rat.

"Do not be afraid, little one," said Hun-Apu.[1] "We will not

---

1. **Hun-Apu** (ho͞on•a'po͞o)

hurt you. You shall go free, as the rest of them have gone"; and he disentangled the little rat and set him on the ground free to go where he would.

"Thank you, thank you!" said the rat. "And now in return for your kindness I will tell you the story of your father and your uncle, that you may be warned, and escape the dread enemy by whose wiles they were destroyed."

Hun-Apu and Xbalanque[2] listened while the rat told them how their father and their uncle had been lured to their death by the lords of Hades, and they vowed to take terrible vengeance on these cruel and treacherous beings. The mention of the game of ball which their father had loved so greatly aroused their keenest interest, for their grandmother in their childhood had kept them

▲ A relief sculpture of a Mayan ballplayer.

---

2. **Xbalanque** (ex'ba•länk'ā)

No Heroic Feet

The ballgame known as "pok-ta-pok" was once popular throughout Central America. It was played for both entertainment and religious purposes, often ending with the sacrifice of one or more players. To play, two teams would gather on an I-shaped stone court with two upright or sloping walls along the sides. The players would hit a large, solid rubber ball with their knees, chests, elbows, and hips, but *not* with their hands or feet. Other rules of the game are still unknown. To score, the players may have had to hit the ball through one of the rings on the walls—a nearly impossible feat. It is more likely that the players hit the ball back and forth and scored points for failed returns. Like football players of today, pok-ta-pok players wore padding to protect themselves from the hard surfaces and from the force of the ball. In imitation of the twins, though, Mayan pok-ta-pok players sported fancy headdresses rather than helmets.

as far as she could from all knowledge of the game, and since they had grown older they had cared for no other pastime than hunting. Now they thought they would like to try the sport that their father had loved.

"The clubs and balls of Hunhun-Apu[3] are hidden away in your grandmother's hut," said the rat. "If you ask her for them she must give them to you."

The twins went home and demanded the clubs and balls that had belonged to their father. Sadly the old woman realized that the day she had so long dreaded was come, and that the gods had decreed that her grandsons should in their turn be drawn to the game that had destroyed their father. Sadly she gave them what they asked for, and from that hour Hun-Apu and Xbalanque lost their former delight in hunting and devoted themselves to the game of ball.

---

3. Hunhun-Apu (ho͞on•ho͞on•a′po͞o)

It was not long before news of this reached the lords of Hades. "Here," they thought, "is our chance to destroy the sons as we destroyed the father."

Once more messengers passed from the dark under-realm to challenge the divinities on earth; and in spite of their grandmother's entreaties and warnings, the brothers accepted the challenge. "Do not fear," they said; "the lords of Hades will not harm us. We shall return to you in triumph, having avenged our father. See, we will plant each a cane in the middle of the hut. Watch these, and while they remain straight and strong you will know that all is well with us; but if they dry up and fall it will be a sign that we are dead."

Shouting a cheerful good-bye to their mother and their grandmother, they set off on the dismal road that leads to Hades.

"Before we go any farther," said Hun-Apu, "let us consider how we can escape the snares which the rat told us were set for our father and uncle. The river of blood which they had to cross will not frighten us. Then there are the wooden images that our father took to be Hun-Came[4] and Vukub-Came,[5] and which he greeted, so that their followers made a jest of him, laughing loudly and rousing him to anger. They shall not make a jest of us, for we will send Xau, the deer, before us as a scout, and he shall prick them all with a hair from my leg, so that he will find out which are real men, and which are made of wood; at the same time he can listen to their talk, and tell us which are really the two lords. When they ask us to sit in the seat of honor we will refuse courteously, knowing that it is in truth a red-hot stone; and our spirits will not sink when we come into the dreadful House of Gloom, for we shall know that for those who are calm and brave it has no terrors."

---

4. **Hun-Came** (hōōn·kä'mä)
5. **Vukub-Came** (vōō·kōōb'kä'mä)

All these things they did, to the very great disappointment of their enemies. Then came the game of ball, and the brothers, playing with easy, laughing confidence, gained a notable victory. More and more angry grew Hun-Came and Vukub-Came, so that they could no longer keep up the pretence of goodwill. They bade the brothers go to the royal garden and

bring back four bouquets, and they secretly instructed the gardeners to allow no flower to be touched. The twins, convinced that some trick was intended, did not attempt to go themselves, but created a great army of ants which swarmed all over the garden and carried off the flowers.

"Take them away to the House of Lances," shouted the angry lords, "and shut them up securely."

The House of Lances was a terrible place, where demons armed with steel lances struck at the prisoners; but Hun-Apu and Xbalanque defended themselves by their arts, and not one of the weapons so much as pierced their skin. They passed triumphantly through the hall, and bribed the owls who guarded the entrance to let them go free.

When the lords of Hades found out that their prisoners had escaped, they were in a fury of rage. They took the owls and slit their beaks in punishment. They pursued and seized Hun-Apu and Xbalanque and made them pass through all the tortures of that dreadful kingdom. One night the brothers were forced to spend in the House of Cold, another in the House of Tigers, and a third in the House of Fire; and from all they returned uninjured. Then their enemies shut them up in the horrible House of Bats, where hateful bat-like creatures with leathern wings and claws like swords made the air dark and fearful. Here the Ruler of the Bats swept down on Hun-Apu, and with cruel claws cut off his head.

Hun-Apu fell lifeless to the ground, and Xbalanque, mad with rage and grief, made furious efforts to reach the loathsome creatures who hovered just beyond his reach, mocking his anguish. At that moment it chanced that a tortoise crawled along the floor, and by chance touched the bleeding neck of Hun-Apu. Immediately the creature became fixed to the place it touched, and rapidly changed into a new head, living and active, just like the one that had been cut off; and Hun-Apu sprang up, not a bit the worse for what had happened.

After this the lords of Hades gave up in despair their efforts to kill these wonder-working gods; and Hun-Apu and Xbalanque called in two sorcerers, by whose help they showed that they were immortal. Both the brothers lay down on biers and died; then the sorcerers ground their bones to powder, and cast the powder into the river. Five days later they made their appearance as creatures partly men and partly fish; the next day they came as ragged old men, and the next in their own proper form. Many other

Counting the Days

The Maya used their knowledge of math and astronomy to develop a calendar. With stunning accuracy, they concluded that one year consisted of 365 days. The Maya, however, divided these days differently than we do. Instead of twelve months, the Maya had eighteen twenty-day months, with five days left over at the end of the year. Each day was associated with a Mayan god, and many months were devoted to different god-related activities. For example, during the first month, Pop, people blessed their useful tools and threw their old ones away. During the eighth month, Mol, beekeepers honored their flowers and bees, while artisans carved new wooden idols. Other months were spent worshipping particular gods.

▲ A section of a Mayan calendar showing the days and rituals.

wonders they did, until the lords of Hades, amazed and crestfallen, felt that the power of which they had been so proud was as nothing compared to the power of these visitors from the upper world. At last their curiosity overcame their dignity, and they cried, "Let us too experience this marvel. Let us be put to death, and then restore our bodies that we may live, and remember what it was like to die."

The brothers saw that here was a chance of ridding themselves of the chief of their enemies. Silently they made a sign to two among the wondering crowd that stood about them. The two stepped forward, and the lords of Hades willingly submitted themselves to the death-stroke. Then Hun-Apu lifted his hand, and cried to the people, "Know all that we are gods from the world above, treacherously ensnared by these your lords, who now lie dead before you. We will not restore them to life. By their own will they died, and their doom is on their own heads. As for you, we will not destroy you, though your deeds have been foul and evil, worthy of death. But through all the future ages you shall be the servants of gods and men; you shall work for them, and the meanest and lowest tasks shall be yours. You shall have power no more over mortals, on the beasts alone shall your magic avail ought. You shall play no more the noble game of ball which you have tried to degrade. Thus the gods punish treachery."

Then Hun-Apu and Xbalanque returned to the upper world, and they set the soul of their father, Hunhun-Apu, and the soul of their uncle, Vukub-Hunapu,[6] in the heavens, and they became the sun and moon, so that all men did them honor.

---

6. **Vukub-Hunapu** (vo͞o•ko͞ob'ho͞on•a'po͞o)

Heroes often seem superhuman simply because they do what no one else dares. In the following Chinese fairy tale, you will see how one young girl takes an ugly matter into her own hands— and proves her worth in the process.

Li Chi Slays the Serpent

KAN PAO

In Fukien,[1] in the ancient state of Yüeh, stands the Yung mountain range, whose peaks sometimes reach a height of many miles. To the northwest there is a cleft in the mountains once inhabited by a giant serpent seventy or eighty feet long and wider than the span of ten hands. It kept the local people in a state of constant terror and had already killed many commandants from the capital city and many magistrates and officers of nearby towns. Offerings of oxen and sheep did not appease the monster. By entering men's dreams and making its wishes known through mediums, it demanded young girls of twelve or thirteen to feast on.

Helpless, the commandant and the magistrates selected daughters of bondmaids[2] or criminals and kept them until

---

1. Fukein (foō'kyen'): province in southeast China.

2. bondmaids: girls or women who serve as bonded servants or slaves.

You Need to Know...

Chinese culture is over three thousand years old. Chinese myths, therefore, reflect the different ways of thinking and living that have taken root in China over this long period of time. Two of the strongest Chinese traditions are Taoism and Confucianism. Both entered Chinese culture between 600 and 300 B.C.

- In Confucianism, the world is centered around an emperor who is favored by the gods. Human beings are arranged in a strict order that gives some people more power than others. In this view, the purpose of all people is to obey those who rule over them.
- By contrast, Taoism holds that all living things are equal. The first Taoists challenged the existing order. They believed that all people possessed certain freedoms, and that the highest purpose of humans is to show compassion.

As you read "Li Chi Slays the Serpent," look for elements of both traditions. In your opinion, which tradition does the story more strongly favor?

the appointed dates. One day in the eighth month of every year, they would deliver a girl to the mouth of the monster's cave, and the serpent would come out and swallow the victim. This continued for nine years until nine girls had been devoured.

In the tenth year the officials had again begun to look for a girl to hold in readiness for the appointed time. A man of Chiang Lo county, Li Tan, had raised six daughters and no sons. Chi, his youngest girl, responded to the search for a victim by volunteering. Her parents refused to allow it, but she said, "Dear parents, you have no one to depend on, for

---

One day in the eighth month of every year, they would deliver a girl to the mouth of the monster's cave, and the serpent would come out and swallow the victim.

---

having brought forth six daughters and not a single son, it is as if you were childless. I could never compare with Ti Jung of the Han Dynasty, who offered herself as a bondmaid to the emperor in exchange for her father's life. I cannot take care of you in your old age; I only waste your good food and clothes. Since I'm no use to you alive, why shouldn't I give up my life a little sooner? What could be wrong in selling me to gain a bit of money for yourselves?" But the father and mother loved her too much to consent, so she went in secret.

The volunteer then asked the authorities for a sharp sword and a snake-hunting dog. When the appointed day of the eighth month arrived, she seated herself in the temple, clutching the sword and leading the dog. First she took several pecks[3] of rice balls moistened with malt sugar and placed them at the mouth of the serpent's cave.

The serpent appeared. Its head was as large as a rice barrel; its eyes were like mirrors two feet across. Smelling the fragrance of the rice balls, it opened its mouth to eat them. Then Li Chi unleashed the snake-hunting dog, which bit hard into the serpent. Li Chi herself came up from behind and scored the serpent with several deep cuts. The wounds hurt so terribly that the monster leaped into the open and died.

Li Chi went into the serpent's cave and recovered the skulls of the nine victims. She sighed as she brought them out, saying, "For your timidity you were devoured. How pitiful!" Slowly she made her way homeward.

The king of Yüeh learned of these events and made Li Chi his queen. He appointed her father magistrate of Chiang Lo county, and her mother and elder sisters were given riches. From that time forth, the district was free of monsters. Ballads celebrating Li Chi survive to this day.

---

3. **pecks:** units of measure for dry products, equal to about eight quarts.

This story comes from Hinduism, the major religion of India. Rama (rä'mə), the story's semi-divine hero, must confront the ten-headed Demon King in order to rescue his kidnapped ladylove. Can he do it? With the right weapons and words—and a little help from his friend Hanuman (hun'o͞o•män')—he just might.

Rama and the Monkey Host

MARGARET JONES

When darkness fell, Bibishana and Hanuman took torches and went to see who had been wounded and bring them help. Much damage had been done, but the monkey general Hanuman, the wind god's son, agreed to go to the northernmost part of India, to the high mountains of the Himalayas, where on one peak grew herbs that could heal even the most terrible of wounds. He swelled to a great size and, leaping into the air, he traveled like the wind to the far, snow-covered peaks. Being in a hurry, he broke off the top of the mountain and carried it swiftly back to Lanka. The skilled doctors amongst the monkey people found the plants they needed and quickly treated the wounded and restored them to full strength. Then the tireless Hanuman picked up the mountaintop and flew back to the

You Need to Know...

Rama, the superhuman hero of this Hindu myth, is the son of the great King Dasaratha. Brave and strong, Rama is the perfect prince. He is also said to be the *avatar* (av'ə•tär'), or human form, of one of Hinduism's major gods, Vishnu (vish'no͞o). Altogether, Vishnu is said to have taken on ten human forms. At birth, Rama was given part of Vishnu's supernatural powers so that he might defeat Ravana, the evil Demon King. When Ravana kidnaps Rama's wife, Sita, and holds her captive on the island of Lanka, Rama becomes enraged. With his brother and a host of monkeys, he crosses the sea and confronts Ravana's mighty demon army. The story you are about to read opens in the midst of this battle, shortly after the gruesome defeat of a monkey-eating giant.

Himalayan range, where he set it once more in place.

The next day Ravana was dismayed to see the monkey host restored and ready to fight again. He sent out his son Indrajit, who was skilled in evil magic and who now bore in his chariot a woman, the very image of Sita. He held her by the hair and, riding up and down the field, threatened to kill her in front of Rama and all the host. Hanuman, horrified by the spectacle, ordered his monkeys to fall back and cease from fighting, and Rama was well-nigh overcome with anguish and uncertainty. But Bibishana, who knew the demon and all his sorcery, said, "Do not lose heart. Indrajit is full of such tricks. Depend upon it, this is only an illusion, and most surely, the true Sita is hidden away safely inside the city."

▲ Hanuman kneels before Rama and his attendants.

The Long and Short of It

The complete adventures of Rama and Sita can be found in a long poem called the *Ramayana* (rä•mä′yə•nə). The *Ramayana* is one of two sacred Hindu texts. The other, the *Mahabharata* (mə•hä′bä′rə•tə), tells the history of the Indian people. The *Ramayana*—all fifty thousand lines of it—was first written down sometime between 200 B.C. and A.D. 200. The people and events first told about were probably real. Over time, though, the characters grew into super-human beings and the events became fantastical. Today, many Hindus look to the *Ramayana* for moral guidance, basing their own actions on those of Rama and Sita. Others simply enjoy telling and retelling the *Ramayana's* colorful tale.

▲ Sita kneeling in a small temple.

So Rama and Lakshman fought with new determination against Ravana's son. Lakshman bore the brunt of that terrible fight, with many severe wounds, but in the end he set an arrow in his bow and whispered over it, "If Rama is righteous and his cause just, then kill this son of Ravana." He let loose the shaft with such force that it severed the demon's head from his body.

Bitterly Ravana grieved for Indrajit, saying, "O my son, it should have been you who performed my funeral rites, not I yours. Now you have gone, with all my war leaders, to be with Yama, who rules over the realm of the dead. I alone am left to face my enemies."

Mounting his great chariot, he rode out onto the battlefield, scattering the monkeys left and right and wielding a deadly weapon in every one of his twenty hands. Seeing his brother Bibishana fighting in Rama's ranks, he angrily cast a weapon at him, but Lakshman flung a javelin that caught and shattered it. Ravana shouted in fury, "Killer of my son, you have protected my brother. Now protect yourself if you can!"

With that he threw a great dart that pierced Lakshman, and he fell to the ground most sorely wounded.

In battle frenzy, Ravana drove on until he came within striking distance of Rama, and the two archenemies faced one another in final battle.

Rama stood tall and long-armed, holding a great bow that seemed to touch the sky. Behind him appeared the gods who keep the Heavenly Weapons, ready to place in his hand any war tool he might wish for. Again and again, the prince's

The Arrow Finds Its Mark

Rama slays Ravana with a bow and arrow—one of the world's oldest weapons. The first known bows and arrows were crafted in western Europe about 40,000 years ago. This invention must have caused quite a stir. Unlike the clumsier spear, the bow and arrow enabled hunters to kill their prey from a distance—swiftly and silently. Early bows, though, were usually made completely of wood. Because wood is not very elastic, these bows often broke when stretched. By the time of the *Ramayana*—about 2,000 years ago—the bow and arrow had been much improved. Bows were now fashioned from elastic materials such as animal sinews, plant fibers, and hair. These flexible bows could store more energy when drawn, and were therefore more deadly when released.

arrows struck off one of Ravana's ten heads, but always another grew straightaway in its place, and the Demon King seemed invincible.

At last Rama said, "Spirits of the Heavenly Weapons, give me a shaft that has the wind in its feathers, the sun and fire in its head."

Immediately a great arrow came into his hand; then it was in his bow, and seconds later, with his prayers upon it, it had found the heart of the Demon King and pierced it through. Ravana's huge trunk crashed to the ground from his chariot; all his ten heads were laid in the dust, and his life was ended. His demon followers dropped their weapons and scattered in disarray.

Great was the satisfaction of the gods when they saw that their purpose had been fulfilled, and great was the joy among all the host that followed Rama. In triumph he entered Lanka and was reunited with faithful Sita. Lakshman's wounds were healed with the powerful Himalayan herbs, and Bibishana was proclaimed King of Lanka in place of his brother.

After some time, when all were rested and refreshed, Rama and his brother Lakshman made preparations to return to the city of Ayodhya, for the fourteen years of Rama's exile were now over, and he was ready to take his rightful place as Rajah. Bibishana insisted that they should travel in a wonderful flying chariot that had belonged to Ravana. It had two stories and made sweet music as it flew through the air, drawn by a flock of golden geese.

Rama invited Bibishana and all the valiant monkeys to go with them and enjoy the hospitality of his city. It was agreed that Hanuman should go ahead to tell Rama's brother Bharata the story of the great victory and let him know that Rama and Sita and Lakshman were coming home. You may be sure that when Bharata heard this news, his joy was unbounded.

Bibishana insisted that they should travel in a wonderful flying chariot. . . . it flew through the air, drawn by a flock of golden geese.

And so they returned to a rapturous welcome. A day was appointed for Rama's coronation, and when that day dawned, a radiant Sita was decked in rich jewels and pearls and clothed in a silken sari. Rama mounted the chariot with his brothers Bharata and Satrughna. Bharata drove, and Satrughna held the royal umbrella over Rama. Lakshman and the demon Bibishana rode beside them, and Sugriva the Monkey King and Hanuman with all the other monkey leaders were mounted on elephants. So with music and the sound of trumpets, they entered the city. Bharata took the sandals from the throne, and Rama and Sita sat on it, side by side, and received their crowns.

Bharata bowed before his brother and said, "Let the world behold you enthroned like the sun at noonday. You will no more dwell in lonely places but sleep and rise to the sound of music and the tinkle of women's anklets. May you rule as long as the sun endures, O Rajah."

And Rama said, "So be it."

The monkeys stayed in Ayodhya for more than a month, feasted and honored by all, until at last they went back to their jungle home, laden with gifts.

The friendship between Rama and the monkey general, Hanuman, lasted as long as they both lived. The Rajah of Ayodhya and Sita his beautiful queen never forgot the help the monkeys had given them when they needed it most.

Hanuman the Monkey God

Because of his selfless devotion to Rama, Hanuman the monkey god is widely loved by Hindus throughout Asia. He is especially important to wrestlers and bodybuilders, who honor the monkey god for his power and strength. Once a year, during the Indian month of Chaitra (parts of March-April), a celebration is held in honor of Hanuman. On this day people make offerings of bananas and sweets to the god. Other, real-life monkeys get lots of treats, too! People play wrestling games and gather at temples to listen to stories about Hanuman. In Thailand, dances, plays, and puppet shows about his adventures are often performed. The actors and dancers in these performances wear elaborate costumes—including masks that symbolize the monkey god's superhuman powers.

If you've ever gotten out of bed to double-check the closet, you know that monsters don't lurk there at night. In the dark world of this Anglo-Saxon tale, though, there *are* things that go bump in the night. Luckily, there's a hero to bump them right back. Read on to meet the larger-than-life Beowulf (bā'ə•wo͞olf')—and his larger-than-life foe, the grisly Grendel (gren'dəl).

The Song of Beowulf

OLIVIA E. COOLIDGE

The lands of King Hrothgar, the Dane, lay at the edge of barren moorlands whose wind-swept ridges echoed with the howling of wolves, the moaning of winds, and the rushing of water. Few ranged this desolate country but huntsmen and wandering shepherds, and of those who had ventured thither, many had never returned. This was the home of the monster, Grendel, who preyed on beasts and men. Some lying close concealed had seen him pass in the moonlight with an aged hag creeping at his heels. They spoke of his shaggy form, resembling a huge, clumsy man, of his fingers like iron claws, of his rolling eyes and hideous countenance, a swollen, purplish red.

Down on the coastal plain the great hall of Hrothgar shone like the golden sun. Its high roof was a landmark for chieftains in many an inlet. The paved road leading to its doorway was set with colored stones. Gold shone

You Need to Know...

The epic *Beowulf* is the oldest known work of literature in Old English. First recorded by an unknown Englishman in about A.D 700, *Beowulf* describes even earlier events in Sweden and Denmark. This fact tells us that the first English people—known as Anglo-Saxons—hailed from lands to the north. The story of Beowulf also shows us that Anglo-Saxons had the same world view as other northern people. Because of their harsh environment, northern people believed that life offered few rewards. There was no afterlife to look forward to—only, if you were lucky, a heroic death. Some comfort could also be found in the strong relationship between king and warrior. Warriors were fiercely loyal to their lords. In exchange, a king cared for his followers and offered them riches.

on the long tables and on the splendid hangings which adorned the walls. The trunk of a whole tree burned in the central hearth, sending its smoke curling up to the high vents in the roof past timbers brightly painted and as yet hardly dimmed by soot. Great tubs of ale stood ready for the feasting, and when the torches were lit, the queen herself bore drink to the nobles, while her women served the rest. Shouting and laughter arose, or in a silence the minstrel would sing of some hero, such as Sigmund, the Volsung, who won the gift of Odin's sword.

Grendel stood on a little knoll at the foot of the hills one evening, staring at the lights in the valley as he listened to the distant sounds of King Hrothgar's feast. Rage and hatred twisted the monster's features. He was waiting until the noises should die and the lights be dimmed. Then he would creep over the pasture and plowland, past the storehouses, up the paved road, and set his great shoulder to the iron-bound doors. He would burst the bars asunder and fall like a savage bear on the sleepers within, as he had often done before. He stirred impatiently in the darkness. There was no moon.

▲ Beowulf vows to destroy Grendel.

The feasting was late in Hrothgar's hall that night, for guests had come to the king from Sweden. Beowulf, the prince of the Geats, had vowed to destroy the horrible monster who was nightly ravaging Hrothgar's hall. His ship had put in to the harbor that day, and now he sat in the high seat of honor, while the queen herself bore him his ale horn. "Welcome, brave guest," she said to him. "It is a great deed of valor that you have sworn to do. None of our men can slay this monster who haunts us, so that it is death to sleep in our hall."

"No sword will pierce him," agreed the aged Hrothgar. "No armor avails against his claws of steel. He is far taller than human and stronger than three men. There is no hero in Denmark who can rid us of this fearsome demon."

As Beowulf lifted his horn, the light shone on his armor of linked mail. He tilted his red head back as he drank, then set down the horn and turned to his host with a smile. "If weapons avail me nothing, I will slay this monster with my bare hands, or die," said he.

Old Hrothgar looked at the huge young man, wondering at his courage as he replied, "Many a one has sworn over the ale-cup that he would kill Grendel. The floor beneath our rushes is red with the blood of these heroes until it seems to me there are no warriors left in Denmark to equal those who have gone. I am old and have seen too much slaughter, yet I will not dissuade you, for I think you are far the strongest man that my eyes have ever beheld."

Monster Madness

Long ago, most people assumed that monsters were real. Although they came in all shapes and sizes, monsters usually had two things in common: they were awful to look at, and they ate humans. Like Grendel, these creatures often seemed to be part animal, part human, and part demon. One of the most widely feared creatures was the dragon, which combined all the most frightening aspects of the serpent, the lizard, the bird, and the crocodile. Dragons were thought to live in water caves, where they hoarded jewels and other stolen treasures. Indeed, when our hero Beowulf is an old man, he slays just such a dragon—and loses his own life in the process.

King Hrothgar drank to his guest, and his men pledged Beowulf's men. Red firelight gleamed on bright helmets, on golden cheek guards, on rows of shields by the entrance, on long spears tipped with iron. Servants bore fresh drink to the tables, while talk and laughter went round. It was late when the king grew weary, but at last he rose. "I shall bid you good night, strangers," he said. "I am old now, but great warriors have served me. I give you my word that no men but my own have ever guarded my hall until now." He motioned to his followers to attend him. Some left with him

---

Red firelight gleamed on bright helmets, on golden cheek guards, on rows of shields by the entrance, on long spears tipped with iron.

---

gladly, some in anger because the old man, appalled by the nights of bloodshed, had bidden his remaining warriors sleep elsewhere.

Beowulf took off his sword and stripped himself of his armor, without which his huge back and arms looked almost gigantic. "Spread bedding for my men," he cried to the servants. "They will wait for the monster with their weapons beside them, but I will face him bare-handed as I am."

Men brought out beds and bolsters. Beowulf's followers laid their shields at their heads, their helmets on the bench above them, and their long spears against the wall. Torches were dimmed, and soon the only sounds were heavy breathing or the tossing of restless men.

Out on the hillside the monster stirred as the lights went out. With a rolling gait like a bear on his hind legs, he moved out of the thickets into the pasture land.

Beowulf lay wakeful, listening. Boards creaked now and then, the glowing fire crackled, wind rustled the hangings. Outside, he could hear no noise.

Suddenly with a mighty crash the door burst inward, and a shaggy form stood in the entrance, filling it from side to side. For a moment, Grendel surveyed the hall, which was dimly lighted by the embers of the fire. Then with a snarl he leaped on one man so quickly that none had time to prevent him. The victim gave a loud cry, which was choked almost as soon as it was uttered and was followed by a hideous, tearing noise. Beowulf lay still in his place, for the man had died in an instant. The others too were quiet, waiting for the movement of their chief.

Grendel stood up from his prey and paused once more as his eyes went round the room. Quickly, Beowulf made a slight motion. The monster saw it and leaped across the floor with a single bound to fall on the hero with his iron claws reaching towards his victim's throat.

All Heroes Great and Small

In 1936, a scholar named J.R.R. Tolkien published an essay about an old, overlooked epic poem called *Beowulf.* His essay brought other scholars running to reexamine the ancient text. Soon, *Beowulf* had soared into the literary spotlight it still enjoys today. Some scholars argue that Tolkien is indebted to *Beowulf.* Indeed, his famous trilogy *The Lord of the Rings* is similar to *Beowulf* in some ways. Both epics share a rustic setting, fantastical creatures, and a heroic theme. However, other scholars point out that the quiet heroism at work in *The Lord of the Rings* is very different from the boastful, superhuman, single-handed heroism of *Beowulf.* In Tolkien's Middle Earth, small, kindly deeds—together with teamwork and cooperation—turn small, humble creatures called Hobbits into very big heroes.

Beowulf scrambled up on one knee. His hands shot out, caught a hairy arm by the wrist, and twisted it sideways. With a fearful crash the monster pitched headfirst onto the floor. Beowulf leaped on his back, still holding the arm. Grendel kicked out, and a bench went flying. He staggered up and whirled to dash his enemy onto a pillar. Beowulf kicked in his turn, and the fiend went thudding against the wall. Boards cracked, shields clattered to the floor, and a hanging sword fell full upon Grendel's back, glancing off his iron hide as though he wore chain armor. With a howl the monster threw himself to the ground and rolled to dislodge his adversary, but Beowulf clung the tighter, and the two went over and over, grasping at tables, tearing at hangings, kicking and clawing. Men sprang to Beowulf's aid, but so dark was the room and so mad the struggle that none dared to strike, lest he wound his master.

▲ Beowulf struggles with Grendel.

At last the two rolled into the center of the floor, and Grendel's cheek fell full on the burning coals. With a horrible cry he leaped up and shook the hero from his back, though he could not free his arm. Now Grendel's iron claws might have torn at his enemy if he had thought to use them, but he was bewildered by the pain of the fire and terrified by the might of the grip which held him. He had no idea but that of flight.

Then followed a fierce tug-of-war down the length of the hall to the doorway. There Beowulf braced his foot behind the door jamb and stood immovable, while Grendel, half in the open, pulled with all his strength. Beowulf twisted the

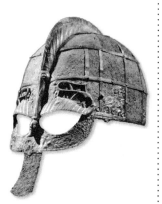

arm savagely. There was a loud snap, and the monster screamed. The hero pulled mightily until with a rending sound the demon's arm broke clean from the socket. He fled moaning into the night, while Beowulf tumbled backward with the grisly trophy pressed close against his breast.

When the sun was up next morning, great bloodstained tracks could be seen marking the path of Grendel's flight. Horsemen followed them rejoicing far into the hills. Hrothgar smiled on the wreck and ruin in his hall as he gave orders to replace the torn hangings, to set up the benches, and renew the iron bands of the doorway. High over the door hung the hand of Grendel, and the trackers saluted it with joyful shouts as they came galloping back from the hills.

The feast that night in Hrothgar's hall was more glorious than ever before. To Beowulf the king gave horses, a saddle set with jewels, and a helmet and breastplate inlaid with gold. The queen came forth in state to bring Beowulf drink and to offer her own gifts, a coat of linked mail and a bright jeweled collar. Men drank to the health of Beowulf's followers, and the king bestowed on them rings of gold. The minstrel sang a lay of the heroes of old, but when he had ended, those next him cried, "Sing us tomorrow a song of Beowulf. His deeds must be remembered among us for as long as this hall shall stand."

Read On

Would you like to read more tales from Northern European lands? Two interesting collections are the classic *Nordic Gods and Heroes* by Padraic Colum (Dover) and *Odin's Family* by Neil Philip (Orchard). A humorous fictionalized account of a theft is found in *Thor's Hammer* by Will Shetterly (Random House Children's).

Connections ▪ A POEM

This verse is taken from an African story about a hero named Liongo. Imprisoned by his enemies, at night he sings songs to the crowd of villagers that gather near his cell—songs, like this one, that celebrate good and put evil to shame. We can still hear his song today in the deeds of our heroes.

▲ Firemen raise an American flag over the rubble of the World Trade Center after both towers collapsed from a terrorist attack.

What is a Hero?
from "Liongo, a Hero of Shanga"

What is a hero but a man who will not turn away
    from what he knows to be right?

He will stand against wrong until his heart becomes still
    and his soul departs.

If he hears an evil thing praised as something good,
    he denounces it and draws his sword.

If evil seeks to hide in the dark shadows of caves,
  he follows and destroys it.

He does not avoid death when it comes, but turns back
  from dying in a false cause.

If his slave stands by his side when he fights a hero's
  fight, his slave too is a hero.

If his enemy stands bravely and fights to the last,
  he praises his enemy as he would praise himself.

But if his enemy stands before him and trembles,
  the hero turns away and does not judge him.

The hero must forever earn merits, even if he has done
  great deeds. He must earn merits again and again.

CHAPTER 3
Perils Along the Way

Hero's Journey

The hero's quest, or journey, is no walk in the park. It must be undertaken without a compass or a road map. The path—when there is one—is riddled with holes and stones. Malicious monsters lurk in the shadowy woods. The temptation to stop, to rest—even to turn around—is great. However, what would a hero be without perils to overcome? And what would we be without heroes to make us stronger and better? After all, the hero's perils are symbols of our own human fears. They show on the *outside* what we all fear on the *inside*: being defeated, being wounded, being kept from our true cause, being without protection or help. By creating heroes, human beings reassure themselves about their own abilities. Our heroes show us that it is possible to defeat the monster, to beat back the fear, to say *no* to the temptation, to follow the true course. The rewards, they promise, will be great—no less than life itself, wisdom, and love. Of course, mythology also serves up a goodly number of heroes who stumble and fall. These heroes teach a different kind of lesson. They do not reassure but rather warn us against our own weakness and folly. "If you go down this path," they caution, "an unhappy consequence will follow."

▲ Luke Skywalker of *Star Wars*.

Memorable Quote

"Heroes take journeys, confront dragons, and discover the treasure of their true selves."

—Carol Pearson
The Hero Within,
HarperCollins, 1986

Big Feet, Tall Tales?

The heroes of this chapter will bring you face-to-face with some downright bloodcurdling creatures. What about the "monsters" that lurk behind modern-day myths?

INVESTIGATE: What are some of the creatures and obstacles that a hero might meet on his or her journey?

- The **Abominable Snowman,** also known as the yeti, is said to roam the highlands of the Himalaya Mountains. This large, hairy biped was first spotted by Europeans in the 1920s. Later, a traveler in 1938 reported that, when he became ill, a nine-foot-tall yeti kindly nursed him back to health! Some experts believe that this "monster" is most likely a savage mountain ape known as the *mih teh.*

- *Sasquatch* is from an American Indian term meaning "wild men." Also known as **Bigfoot,** this humanlike creature of the Pacific Northwest is said to sport a shaggy coat, walk on two feet, and avoid human company. According to reports, he measures six to fifteen feet tall, weighs about six-hundred and fifty pounds, and leaves super-sized footprints. Most scientists, though, doubt that such a beast exists.

- The beloved **Loch Ness monster** is said to navigate the waters of a Scottish *loch,* or lake. First written about in A.D. 565, "Nessie" is often likened to a dinosaur or a sea serpent, and some believe her to be a throwback to prehistoric times. Over the years, cameras and other devices have supposedly captured images of Nessie. The most famous (see left) was proved in 1993 to be a hoax—a toy submarine fitted with a sea-monster head. Still, the Nessie legend continues to float.

Heroes aren't perfect. They often stumble on the road to great-ness, and sometimes their mistakes can prove fatal. As you read about the hero Theseus (the'sōōs'), look for a flaw in his character. How might this lead to his downfall?

Theseus and the Minotaur

ROBERT GRAVES

On a visit to Corinth, King Aegeus of Athens secretly married the Princess Aethra. She had grown tired of waiting for Bellerophon,[1] whose wife she should have been, to come home from Lydia. After a few pleasant days with Aethra, Aegeus told her: "I am afraid I must leave now, my dear. It will be safest, in case you have a son, to pre-tend that his father is the God Poseidon.[2] My eldest nephew might kill you if he knew of our marriage. He expects to be the next King of Athens. Goodbye!"

Once back, Aegeus never left Athens again.

Aethra had a son whom she named Theseus, and on his four-teenth birthday she asked him: "Can you move that huge rock?" Theseus, a remarkably strong boy, lifted the rock and

---

1. Bellerophon (bə•ler'ə•fän'): The Greek hero Bellerophon rode the winged horse Pegasus and killed a fire-breathing monster called the Chimera.

2. Poseidon (pō•si'dən): one of the Olympians, the twelve major Greek gods and goddesses. Poseidon, called Neptune by the Romans, was the god of the sea and of horses.

You Need to Know...

The myth of Theseus and the Minotaur (min'ə•tôr') is probably based on actual events. In ancient times the island of Crete (krēt) was home to an advanced civilization that boasted grand palaces, beautiful artworks—even indoor plumbing. The Cretan king-dom of Knossus (näs'əs) was ruled by a king called Minos. Minos was known to wear the head of a bull for important events. His palace was a vast, rambling structure with numerous rooms, floors, and passages. There, every eight or nine years, human sacrifices are thought to have been made. Eventually the island of Crete was invaded by Mycenaeans (mī'sə•nē'ənz) from the north. When they stormed the palace in search of the king, the Mycenaeans were probably confused by its size and its mazelike structure. Forced into battle, Minos almost certainly wore his bullish headdress—although it did not save him from defeat. As you read the story of Theseus, look for mythical events that mirror these historical ones.

tossed it away. Hidden underneath, he found a sword with a golden snake pattern inlaid on the blade, and a pair of sandals. "Those were left there by your father," Aethra said. "He is Aegeus, King of Athens. Take them to him and say that you found them under this rock. But mind, not a word to his nephews, who will be furious if they discover that you are the true heir to the throne of Athens. Because of them I have pretended all these years that Poseidon, not Aegeus, was your father."

Theseus went by the coast road to Athens. First he met a giant named Sinis, who had the horrible habit of bending two pine trees down towards each other, tying some poor traveler to their tops by his arms, and then suddenly letting go. The trees would fly upright and tear him in two. Theseus wrestled with Sinis, threw him senseless on the ground, and then treated him as he had treated others.

Next, Theseus faced and killed a monstrous wild sow, with tusks larger and sharper than sickles. Then he fought Procrustes, a wicked innkeeper who lived beside the main road and kept only one bed in his inn. If travelers were too short for the bed, Procrustes would lengthen them with an instrument of torture called "the rack"; if they were too tall, he would chop off their feet; and if they were the right size, he would smother them with a blanket. Theseus beat

Procrustes, tied him to the bed, and cut off both his feet; but, finding him still too tall, cut off his head as well. He wrapped the dead body in a blanket and flung it into the sea.

King Aegeus had recently been married again: to a witch named Medea. Theseus did not know about this marriage, yet on his arrival at Athens, Medea knew by magic who he was; and decided to poison him—putting wolfbane[3] in a cup of wine. She wanted one of her own sons to be the next King. Luckily Aegeus noticed the snake pattern on Theseus' sword, guessed that the wine had been poisoned, and hastily knocked the cup from Medea's hand. The poison burned a large hole through the floor, and Medea escaped in a magic cloud. Then Aegeus sent a chariot to fetch Aethra from Corinth, and announced: "Theseus is my son and heir." The next day, Aegeus's nephews ambushed Theseus on his way to a temple; but he fought and killed them all.

Now, it had happened some years before that King Minos's son, Androgeus of Crete, visited Athens and there won all the competitions in the Athletic Games—running, jumping, boxing, wrestling, and throwing the discus. Aegeus's jealous nephews accused him of a plot to seize the throne, and murdered him. When Minos complained about this to the Olympians, they gave orders that Aegeus must send seven boys and seven girls from Athens every ninth year to be devoured by the Cretan Minotaur. The Minotaur was a monster—half bull, half man—which Minos kept in the middle of the Labyrinth, or maze, built for him by Daedalus. The Minotaur knew every twist and turn in the Labyrinth, and would chase his victims into some blind alley where he had them at his mercy.

So now the Athenians, angry with Theseus for killing his cousins, chose him as one of the seven boys sent to be eaten that year. Theseus thanked them, saying that he was glad of a chance to free his country of this horrid tribute. The ship in

---

3. **wolfbane,** or wolfsbane: a poisonous plant of the buttercup family, with hoodlike yellow flowers.

which the victims sailed carried black sails, for mourning, but Theseus took white sails along, too. "If I kill the Minotaur, I shall hoist these white sails. If the Minotaur kills me, let the black ones be hoisted."

Theseus prayed to the Goddess Aphrodite.[4] She listened to him and told her son Eros[5] to make Ariadne, Minos's daughter, fall in love with Theseus. That same night, she came to Theseus' prison, drugged the guards, unlocked the door of his cell with a key stolen from Minos's belt, and asked Theseus: "If I help you to kill the Minotaur, will you marry me?"

"With pleasure," he answered, kissing her hand.

Ariadne led the boys quietly from the prison. She showed them a magic ball of thread, given her by Daedalus before he left Crete. One need only tie the loose end of the thread to the Labyrinth door, and the ball would roll by itself through all the twisting paths until it reached the clear space in the middle. "The Minotaur lives there," Ariadne said. "He sleeps for exactly one hour in the twenty-four, at midnight; but then he sleeps sound."

Theseus' six companions kept guard at the entrance, while Ariadne tied the thread to the Labyrinth door. Theseus

A-Maze-Ing Labyrinths

It is doubtful that Daedalus's (ded''l•əs) bullpen labyrinth actually existed. However, some historical labyrinths are still with us today.

The Egyptians built a labyrinth that contained 3,000 chambers—1,500 above ground and 1,500 below.

The floors of some French cathedrals were inlaid with tile or stone labyrinths that symbolized the religious pilgrim's journey.

An old garden maze still exists in England's Hampton Court Palace. The leafy walls of the maze are hedges of holly and yew. To reach the center, you must take a left, two rights, and then a series of lefts.

▲ A Cretan coin showing a classical labyrinth.

---

4. **Aphrodite** (af'rə•dīt'ē): the Greek goddess of love and beauty, called Venus by the Romans.

5. **Eros** (er'äs'): the god of love, called Cupid by the Romans.

▲ Theseus using Ariadne's thread to find his way through the labyrinth.

entered, ran his hand along the thread in the darkness and came upon the sleeping Minotaur just after midnight. As the moon rose, he cut off the monster's head with a razor-sharp sword lent him by Ariadne, then followed the thread back to the entrance where his friends stood anxiously waiting. Meanwhile, Ariadne had freed the seven girls, too, and all together they stole down to the harbor. Theseus and his friends, having first bored holes in the sides of Minos's ships, climbed aboard their own, pushed her off, and sailed for Athens. The Cretan ships which gave chase soon filled and sank; so Theseus got safely away, with the Minotaur's head and Ariadne.

Theseus beached his ship on the island of Naxos; he needed food and water. While Ariadne lay resting on the beach, the God Dionysus[6] suddenly appeared to Theseus. "I want

---

6. Dionysus (dī'ə•nī'səs): the Greek god of wine and celebration, called Bacchus by the Romans.

to marry this woman myself," he said. "If you take her from me, I will destroy Athens by sending all its people mad."

Theseus dared not offend Dionysus and, since he had no great love for Ariadne anyway, he left her asleep and set sail. Ariadne wept with rage on waking, to find herself deserted; but Dionysus soon walked up, introduced himself, and offered her a large cup of wine. Ariadne drank it all, felt better at once, and decided that it would be far more glorious to marry a god than a mortal. Dionysus' wedding present to her was the splendid jeweled coronet which is now the constellation called "The Northern Crown." She bore several children to Dionysus, and eventually returned to Crete as Queen.

In the excitement, Theseus had quite forgotten to change the sails, and King Aegeus, watching anxiously from a cliff at Athens, saw the black sail appear instead of the white. Overcome by grief, he jumped into the sea and drowned. Theseus then became King of Athens and made peace with the Cretans.

A few years later, the Amazons, a fierce race of fighting women from Asia, invaded Greece and attacked Athens. Since Theseus listened to the Goddess Athene's[7] advice, he managed to defeat them; but never afterwards stopped boasting about his courage.

One day his friend Peirithous said to him: "I am in love with a beautiful woman. Will you help me to marry her?"

---

7. **Athene** (ə•thē'nē), also called Athena (-nə): the Greek goddess of wisdom, warfare, and crafts.

"By all means," Theseus answered. "Am I not the bravest king alive? Look what I did to the Amazons! Look what I did to the Minotaur! Who is the woman?"

"Persephone, Demeter's[8] daughter," Peirithous answered.

"Oh! Are you serious? Persephone is already married to King Hades, God of the Dead!"

"I know, but she hates Hades and wants children. She can have no living children by the God of the Dead."

"It seems rather a risky adventure," said Theseus, turning pale.

"Are you not the bravest king alive?"

"I am."

"Let us go, then!"

They buckled on their swords and descended to Tartarus[9] by the side entrance. Having given the dog Cerberus[10] three

---

8. **Demeter** (di•mēt'ər): the Greek goddess of fruits, grains, and fertility; her daughter Persephone was abducted against her will by Hades, ruler of the underworld.

9. **Tartarus** (tär'tə•rəs): the Greek underworld, ruled by Hades.

10. **Cerberus** (sʉr'bər•əs): a hideous three-headed dog that guards the gate of Tartarus.

The Case of the Absent Amazons

Ancient Greeks believed that only fierce and warlike women called the Amazons lived in a nearby region known as Amazonia. In battle the Amazons were said to wear helmets, carry shields, and wield double axes and bows. However, when the Greeks actually reached Amazonia, there was nobody there. What had become of the terrible Amazons? And so a new myth was born—that the Greek hero Heracles, along with Theseus, had conquered the warrior women and sent them away. The heroes' rewards? Heracles won the heart of the Amazon queen, Hippolyta, and Theseus took the Amazon princess Antiope back to Athens as his bride.

cakes dipped in poppy juice, to send him asleep, Peirithous rapped at the palace gate and entered.

Hades asked in surprise: "Who are you mortals, and what do you want?"

Theseus told him: "I am Theseus, the bravest king alive. This is my friend Peirithous, who thinks that Queen Persephone is far too good for you. He wants to marry her himself."

Hades grinned at them. Nobody had ever seen him grin before. "Well," he said, "it is true that Persephone is not exactly happy with me. I might even let her go, if you promise to treat her kindly. Shall we talk the matter over quietly? Please, sit down on that comfortable bench!"

▲ Cerberus.

Theseus and Peirithous sat down, but the bench Hades had offered them was a magic one. They became attached to it, so that they could never escape without tearing away part of themselves. Hades stood and roared for laughter, while the Furies[11] whipped the two friends; and ghostly spotted snakes stung them; and Cerberus, waking from his drugged sleep, gnawed at their fingers and toes.

"My poor fools," chuckled Hades, "you are here for always!"

---

11. **Furies:** three female spirits who punish wrongdoers; the Furies have hair made of snakes.

Read On

Follow the fabulous adventures of other heroes in *Greek Myths* by Olivia Coolidge (Houghton Mifflin) and *Tales of the Greek Heroes* by Roger Lancelyn Green (Puffin). Read an account of another hero's adventure in *Odysseus in the Serpent Maze* by Jane Yolen and Robert J. Harris (HarperCollins).

Heroes often make great sacrifices in order to gain what they seek. In this Norse myth the great god Odin poses as an ordinary man—who's not quite so ordinary after all. Read on to learn what Odin surrenders in exchange for a single, eye-opening sip from Mimir's Well.

Odin Goes to Mimir's Well

PADRAIC COLUM

And so Odin,[1] no longer riding on Sleipner,[2] his eight-legged steed; no longer wearing his golden armor and his eagle-helmet, and without even his spear in his hand, traveled through Midgard,[3] the World of Men, and made his way toward Jötunheim,[4] the Realm of the Giants.

No longer was he called Odin All-Father, but Vegtam the Wanderer. He wore a cloak of dark blue and he carried a traveler's staff[5] in his hands. And now, as he went toward Mimir's[6] Well, which was near to Jötunheim, he came upon a Giant riding on a great Stag.

Odin seemed a man to men and a giant to giants. He went beside the Giant on the great Stag and the two talked together. "Who art thou, O brother?" Odin asked the Giant.

---

1. **Odin** (ō'din).
2. **Sleipner** (slāp'nîr).
3. **Midgard** (mid'gärd').
4. **Jötunheim** (yô'tɔon‧hām').
5. **staff:** large stick.
6. **Mimir** (mē'mir').

You Need to Know...

In Norse mythology, Odin, the sky-father, rules over gods and mortals alike. With the help of his two brothers, Odin is said to have killed the giant Ymir (ē'mir) and then used his bones and flesh to create the universe. Luckily, Odin has the power to change shape at will. This power helps protect him from other unfriendly giants. It also enables him to wander creation in search of wisdom. To learn the secrets of life, Odin takes on many different forms: an insect, a leaf, water, wind, and fire, to name a few. Odin also likes to appear as an ordinary human traveler. Sometimes known as Woden (wōd''n) or Wotan, Odin is usually pictured astride his eight-legged steed, Sleipner, or as a blue-cloaked wanderer with a broad-brimmed hat and an eye patch—the origins of which you will shortly learn.

▲ Odin.

"I am Vafthrudner, the wisest of the Giants," said the one who was riding on the Stag. Odin knew him then. Vafthrudner was indeed the wisest of the Giants, and many went to strive to gain wisdom from him. But those who went to him had to answer the riddles Vafthrudner asked, and if they failed to answer the Giant took their heads off.

"I am Vegtam the Wanderer," Odin said, "and I know who thou art, O Vafthrudner. I would strive to learn something from thee."

The Giant laughed, showing his teeth. "Ho, ho," he said, "I am ready for a game with thee. Dost thou know the stakes? My head to thee if I cannot answer any question thou wilt ask. And if thou canst not answer any question that I may ask, then thy head goes to me. Ho, ho, ho. And now let us begin."

"I am ready," Odin said.

"Then tell me," said Vafthrudner, "tell me the name of the river that divides Asgard from Jötunheim?"

"Ifling is the name of that river," said Odin. "Ifling that is dead cold, yet never frozen."

"Thou hast answered rightly, O Wanderer," said the Giant. "But thou hast still to answer other questions. What are the names of the horses that Day and Night drive across the sky?"

"Skinfaxe and Hrimfaxe," Odin answered. Vafthrudner was startled to hear one say the names that were known only to the Gods and to the wisest of the Giants. There was only one question now that he might ask before it came to the stranger's turn to ask him questions.

"Tell me," said Vafthrudner, "what is the name of the plain on which the last battle will be fought?"

"The Plain of Vigard," said Odin, "the plain that is a hundred miles long and a hundred miles across."

It was now Odin's turn to ask Vafthrudner questions. "What will be the last words that Odin will whisper into the ear of Baldur, his dear son?" he asked.

Very startled was the Giant Vafthrudner at that question. He sprang to the ground and looked at the stranger keenly.

"Only Odin knows what his last words to Baldur will be," he said, "and only Odin would have asked that question. Thou art Odin, O Wanderer, and thy question I cannot answer."

"Then," said Odin, "if thou wouldst keep thy head, answer me this: what price will Mimir ask for a draught[7] from the Well of Wisdom that he guards?"

"He will ask thy right eye as a price, O Odin," said Vafthrudner.

"Will he ask no less a price than that?" said Odin.

"He will ask no less a price. Many have come to him for a draught from the Well of Wisdom, but no one yet has given the price Mimir asks. I have answered thy question, O Odin. Now give up thy claim to my head and let me go on my way."

"I give up my claim to thy head," said Odin. Then

---

7. **draught** (draft): an amount of liquid for drinking.

Week's Roll Call

Without realizing it, you probably refer to Odin at least once a week. Several of our weekdays are named after ancient Norse gods, while others come from the ancient Romans. Here is the week's roll call:

Sunday means "Sun's-day." In A.D. 321, the Roman emperor Constantine established the seven-day calendar. He named the first day of the week after the brightest of heavenly bodies.

Monday, or "Moon's-day," was named by the Romans for the gentler heavenly orb.

Tuesday, or "Tyr's-day," is named for Tyr (tir), the Norse god of war.

Wednesday, meaning "Woden's-day," gets its name from Odin. Also known as Woden, this Norse god had several different names as well as shapes.

Thursday, or "Thor's-day," is named after the Norse god of thunder.

Friday, "Frigg's-day," inherits its name from Odin's wife, Frigg.

Saturday means "Saturn's-day." It was named after the Roman god and the planet that bears his name.

Vafthrudner, the wisest of the Giants, went on his way, riding on his great Stag.

It was a terrible price that Mimir would ask for a draught from the Well of Wisdom, and very troubled was Odin All-Father when it was revealed to him. His right eye! For all time to be without the sight of his right eye! Almost he would have turned back to Asgard, giving up his quest for wisdom.

He went on, turning neither to Asgard nor to Mimir's Well. And when he went toward the South he saw Muspelheim, where stood Surtur with the Flaming Sword, a terrible figure, who would one day join the Giants in their war against the Gods. And when he turned North he heard the roaring of the cauldron[8] Hvergelmer as it poured itself out of Niflheim, the place of darkness and dread. And Odin knew that the world must not be left between Surtur, who would destroy it with fire, and Niflheim, that would gather it back to Darkness and Nothingness. He, the eldest of the Gods, would have to win the wisdom that would help to save the world.

And so, with his face stern in front of his loss and pain, Odin All-Father turned and went toward Mimir's Well. It was under the great root of Ygdrassil[9]—the root that grew out of Jötunheim. And there sat Mimir, the Guardian of the

---

8. **cauldron** (kôl'drən), also caldron: a large container.

9. **Ygdrassil** (ig'drə•sil'): ash tree that supports all levels of the Norse universe.

Well of Wisdom, with his deep eyes bent upon the deep water. And Mimir, who had drunk every day from the Well of Wisdom, knew who it was that stood before him.

"Hail, Odin, Eldest of the Gods," he said.

Then Odin made reverence to Mimir, the wisest of the world's beings. "I would drink from your well, Mimir," he said.

"There is a price to be paid. All who have come here to drink have shrunk from paying that price. Will you, Eldest of the Gods, pay it?"

"I will not shrink from the price that has to be paid, Mimir," said Odin All-Father.

"Then drink," said Mimir. He filled up a great horn with water from the well and gave it to Odin.

Odin took the horn in both his hands and drank and drank. And as he drank all the future became clear to him. He saw all the sorrows and troubles that would fall upon

Puzzling Questions

Vafthrudner was not onto something new—riddles have been around for a long time and have often been used as a test.

One type of riddle describes something in a purposefully puzzling way. "What runs around all day and lies under the bed at night?" (answer: your shoes) is an example of this kind of riddle.

Another type of riddle asks cunning or amusing questions and has been around since ancient times. To save his life, the Greek hero Oedipus answered such a riddle posed by the legendary Sphinx: *What walks on four legs in the morning, two at noon, and three in the evening?* (answer: a man, who crawls as a baby, walks as an adult, and uses a cane in old age.)

A more modern, and less lethal, riddle may contain a pun, or play on words—"What is black and white and red all over?"—with red (read) being the tricky word. (answer: a newspaper or an embarrassed zebra!)

Men and Gods. But he saw, too, why the sorrows and troubles had to fall, and he saw how they might be borne so that Gods and Men, by being noble in the days of sorrow and trouble, would leave in the world a force that one day, a day that was far off indeed, would destroy the evil that brought terror and sorrow and despair into the world.

Then when he had drunk out of the great horn that Mimir had given him, he put his hand to his face and he plucked out his right eye. Terrible was the pain that Odin All-Father endured. But he made no groan nor moan. He bowed his head and put his cloak before his face, as Mimir took the eye and let it sink deep, deep into the water of the Well of Wisdom. And there the Eye of Odin stayed, shining up through the water, a sign to all who came to that place of the price that the Father of the Gods had paid for his wisdom.

Rune Boon

Much of Odin's wisdom is earned by suffering. In another story, Odin hangs on Yggdrasil, the world tree, for nine nights, pierced with a spear. At the end of the ordeal, Odin gives a great cry and falls dead from the tree—seizing, as he does so, the knowledge of the runes. The word *rune* comes from an Old Norse word meaning "secret." When he came back to life, Odin is said to have passed the knowledge of the runes on to men. Scholars, though, give more factual explanations of this mysterious alphabet, also known as *futhark*. The alphabet was used by northern Europeans from about A.D. 200 to about 1500 or 1600. It may have been developed by the Goths, an early Germanic people, and was probably based on alphabets from southern Europe. Archaeologists have discovered thousands of runic inscriptions in Sweden, most of them carved in stone or wood between A.D. 800 and 1000—the Viking period.

▼ Stone with runes.

How far would you go to save a friend's life? This excerpt from an ancient Mesopotamian myth might prompt you to rethink the idea of friendship—and the idea that heroes always succeed by their single-handed efforts.

The Monster Humbaba

BERNARDA BRYSON

Gilgamesh and Enkidu walked toward the mountain of the cedar forest. At a distance of twenty double-hours they sat down beside the path and ate a small amount of food. At a distance of thirty double-hours, they lay down to sleep, covering themselves with their garments. On the following day they walked a distance of fifty double-hours. Within three days' time, they covered a distance that it would have taken ordinary men some fifteen days to cover. They reached the mountain and saw before them a towering and magnificent gate of cedar wood.

"Here," said Gilgamesh, "we must pour meal[1] upon the earth, for that will gain us the good-will of the gods; it will persuade them to reveal their purpose in our dreams."

They poured meal on the ground and lay down to sleep.

---

1. **meal** (mēl): a coarsely ground grain.

You Need to Know...

This story comes from a region of the ancient world known as Mesopotamia. The heart of this region lay between the Tigris and Euphrates rivers, and was home to the earliest human civilizations. One of these civilizations, Babylonia, gave birth to a king named Gilgamesh (gil'gə•mesh') in around 2700 B.C. Over time, legends grew up around this king. Thought to be two-thirds god and one-third human, Gilgamesh was exceedingly brave. However, he could also be exceedingly cruel. Weary of being slaves in his kingdom, Gilgamesh's people prayed to the gods for help. In response, the gods sent a wild man, Enkidu (en'kē•doo), to fight Gilgamesh. During the midst of the fight, though, the two superhumans became friends, and the gods' plan was foiled. The excerpt you are about to read begins as Gilgamesh and Enkidu set out to find and slay the monster Humbaba—yet another trap laid by the exasperated gods. In spite of Enkidu's warnings, Gilgamesh is determined, and so onward the two travel toward the monster's mountain home.

After some time Gilgamesh wakened his friend. "Enkidu, I have had a dream; it went like this: We were standing in a deep gorge beside a mountain. Compared to it, we were the size of flies! Before our very eyes the mountain collapsed; it fell in a heap!"

"The meaning of that seems very clear," said Enkidu. "It means that Humbaba is the mountain and that he will fall before us!"

They closed their eyes again and slept. After some time, Gilgamesh again awakened his friend. "I've had another dream, Enkidu. I saw the same mountain this time, and again it fell, but it fell on me. However, as I lay struggling, a beautiful personage appeared. He took me by my feet and dragged me out from under the mountain. Now I wonder what this means? Is it that you will rescue me from the monster, or will someone else come along?"

They pondered a little and went back to sleep. Next Enkidu wakened his brother, Gilgamesh. "Has a cold shower passed over us? Did the lightning strike fires, and was there a rain of ashes?"

"The earth is dry and clean," said Gilgamesh, "you must have dreamed!" But since neither of them could understand the meaning of this dream, they fell asleep again, and soon the day came.

They approached the magnificent gate. "Let's open it, Enkidu! Let's be on our way!"

For a last time, Enkidu tried to persuade his friend to turn back.

▲ A terra-cotta mask of Humbaba.

But since the King would not listen, it was he who went first and placed his hand against the gate to push it open. Enkidu was thrown backward with such violence that he fell to the earth. He rose to his feet. "Gilgamesh, wait! My hand is paralyzed!"

"Put it on my arm, Enkidu! It will take strength from my arm because I am not afraid."

When the two friends threw their weight against the gate, however, it swung inward.

They walked up the mountainside through the sacred trees. And these became closer and thicker until the sky was blotted out. They could hear the giant heartbeat of Humbaba and smell the smoke from his lungs.

To show his daring, Gilgamesh cut one of the cedar trees. The blows of his axe rang out, and from afar the terrible Humbaba heard the sound.

With a crashing of timbers and a rolling of loose stones, Humbaba came down upon them. His face loomed among the tree tops, creased and grooved like some ancient rock. The breath he breathed withered the boughs of cedar and set small fires everywhere.

Enkidu's fears now vanished and the two heroes stood side by side as the monster advanced. He loomed over them, his arms swinging out like the masts of a ship. He was almost upon them when suddenly the friends stepped apart. The giant demon lurched through the trees, stum-

A Hop, Skip, and a Jump

Measuring great distances has always been an inexact science. From the earliest days, human beings have measured things in relation to themselves and the objects around them. The ancient Egyptians, for example, used a unit of measurement called the cubit. It was defined as the distance between the tip of a man's middle finger and his elbow. For the ancient Romans a pace was two steps, and a mile was equal to one thousand paces. In the Middle Ages a rod was determined by lining up the left feet of sixteen men, heel to toe; one-sixteenth of this distance was a foot. The yard (from the word *gierd*, meaning "twig") was the length of a man's arm.

▲ Gilgamesh is often shown fighting wild animals. Here, he is shown taming a lion.

bled, and fell flat. He rose to his feet bellowing like a bull and charged upon Enkidu. But the King brought down his axe on the toe of Humbaba so that he whirled about roaring with pain. He grasped Gilgamesh by his flowing hair, swung him round and round as if to hurl him through the treetops, but now Enkidu saw his giant ribs exposed and he thrust his sword into the monster's side. Liquid fire gushed from the wound and ran in small streams down the mountain-side. Gilgamesh fell to the earth and lay still, trying to breathe. But meanwhile Humbaba grasped the horns of Enkidu and began to flail his body against a tree.

Surely the wild man would have died, but now Gilgamesh roused himself. He lanced into the air his long spear with its handle of lapis lazuli[2] and gold. The spear caught Humbaba in the throat and remained there poised and glittering among the fires that had ignited everywhere.

The giant loosened his hold on Enkidu; he cried out. The earth reverberated with the sound, and distant mountains shook.

---

2. **lapis lazuli** (lap'is laz'yoo•li'): a semiprecious stone, usually deep blue in color.

Gilgamesh felt pity in his heart. He withdrew his sword and put down his axe, while the monster Humbaba crept toward him grovelling and wailing for help. Now Enkidu perceived that the monster drew in a long breath in order to spew forth his last weapon—the searing fire that would consume the King. He leaped on the demon and with many sword thrusts released the fire, so that it bubbled harmlessly among the stones.

Humbaba was dead; the two heroes, black with soot and dirt, were still alive. They hugged each other, they leaped about; and singing and shouting, they descended the mountainside. Gentle rains fell around them and the land was forever free from the curse of the giant Humbaba.

The Cutting Wedge

The Gilgamesh story was first written down in about 2000 B.C. This text was lost, but we do have another one dating back to the 600s B.C. It was inscribed on a set of twelve clay tablets for the library of an Assyrian king, Ashurbanipal. (His was the first organized library in the ancient Middle East.) The twelve tablets—among thousands of others—were discovered over 150 years ago during the excavation of the ancient city of Ninevah. The Gilgamesh tablets contain about 2,900 lines of writing known as cuneiform (kyo͞o•nē'ə•fôrm'). Cuneiform was the most widely used form of writing in the ancient Middle East. It could vary from region to region, sometimes using only a few characters and other times using hundreds. However, all forms had some shared traits. Unlike earlier picture writing, cuneiform characters could stand for words or syllables. These characters were made by pressing a wedge-shaped tool called a stylus into wet clay. Some characters were made of a single wedge, while others were made of thirty or more. Indeed, the technique is so interesting that *cuneiform*, which literally means "wedge-shaped," was named for it.

What makes a hero: reaching a goal, or striving for it? In this Zuni legend, you will meet a hero who stumbles on the path to greatness, but who also teaches us an important lesson.

The Spirit Wife

RETOLD BY RICHARD ERDOES AND ALFONSO ORTIZ

A young man was grieving because the beautiful young wife whom he loved was dead. As he sat at the graveside weeping, he decided to follow her to the Land of the Dead. He made many prayer sticks and sprinkled sacred corn pollen. He took a downy eagle plume[1] and colored it with red earth color. He waited until nightfall, when the spirit of his departed wife came out of the grave and sat beside him. She was not sad, but smiling. The spirit-maiden told her husband: "I am just leaving one life for another. Therefore do not weep for me."

"I cannot let you go," said the young man, "I love you so much that I will go with you to the land of the dead."

The spirit-wife tried to dissuade him, but could not overcome his determination. So at last she gave in to his wishes, saying: "If you must follow me, know that I shall be invisible to you as long as the sun shines. You must tie this red eagle plume to my hair. It will be

---

You Need to Know...

The Zuni (zōō'nē) people have lived on the Arizona-New Mexico border since about A.D. 700. Spanish explorers gave them the name *Zuni*. However, these people refer to themselves as *Ashiwi*, which comes from a word meaning "flesh." The Zuni believe that spirits protect humans and grant them health and long life. These spirits sometimes visit humans, but usually dwell in a village at the bottom of the Lake of the Dead. This lake, in turn, is thought to lie at the bottom of an actual lake near the Colorado River. Many modern-day Zuni keep their ancient beliefs alive and prefer to live apart from the modern world. However, their beautiful pottery and jewelry are in high demand. These items were once used in trade with other tribes. Today they are sold to art lovers throughout the world.

---

1. **plume** (plōōm): a feather.

visible in daylight, and if you want to come with me, you must follow the plume."

The young husband tied the red plume to his spirit-wife's hair, and at daybreak, as the sun slowly began to light up the world, bathing the mountaintops in a pale pink light, the spirit-wife started to fade from his view. The lighter it became, the more the form of his wife dissolved and grew transparent, until at last it vanished altogether. But the red plume did not disappear. It waved before the young man, a mere arms-length away, and then, as if rising and falling on a dancer's head, began leading the way out of the village, moving through the streets out into the cornfields, moving through a shallow stream, moving into the foothills of the mountains, leading the young husband ever westward toward the land of the evening.

The red plume moved swiftly, evenly, floating without effort over the roughest trails, and soon the young man had trouble following it. He grew tireder and tireder and finally was totally exhausted as the plume left him farther behind. Then he called out, panting: "Beloved wife, wait for me. I can't run any longer."

The red plume stopped, waiting for him to catch up, and when he did so, hastened on. For many days the young man traveled, following the plume by day, resting during the nights, when his spirit-bride would sometimes appear to him, speaking encouraging words. Most of the time, however, he was merely aware of her presence in some mysterious way. Day by day the trail became rougher and rougher. The days were long, the nights short, and the young man grew wearier and wearier, until at last he had hardly enough strength to set one foot before the other.

One day the trail led to a deep, almost bottomless chasm,[2] and as the husband came to its edge, the red plume began to float away from him into nothingness. He reached out to seize it, but the plume was already beyond his reach, floating straight across the canyon, because spirits can fly through the air.

The young man called across the chasm: "Dear wife of mine, I love you. Wait!"

He tried to descend one side of the canyon, hoping to climb up the opposite side, but the rock walls were sheer, with nothing to hold onto. Soon he found himself on a ledge barely wider than a thumb, from which he could go neither forward nor back. It seemed that he must fall into the abyss and be dashed into pieces. His foot had already begun to slip, when a tiny striped squirrel scooted up the cliff, chattering: "You young fool, do you think you have the wings of a bird or the feet of a spirit? Hold on for just a little while and I'll help you." The little creature reached into its cheek pouch and brought out a little seed, which it moistened with saliva and stuck into a crack in the wall. With his tiny feet the squirrel danced above the crack, singing: "Tsithl, tsithl, tsithl, tall stalk, tall stalk, tall stalk, sprout, sprout quickly." Out of the crack sprouted a long, slender stalk, growing quickly in length and breadth, sprouting leaves and tendrils, spanning the chasm so that the young man could cross over without any trouble.

---

2. **chasm** (kaz'əm): a deep gap; a canyon.

On the other side of the canyon, the young man found the red plume waiting, dancing before him as ever. Again he followed it at a pace so fast that it often seemed that his heart would burst. At last the plume led him to a large, dark, deep lake, and the plume plunged into the water to disappear below the surface. Then the husband knew that the spirit land lay at the bottom of the lake. He was in despair because he could not follow the plume into the deep. In vain did he call for his spirit-wife to come back. The surface of the lake remained undisturbed and unruffled like a sheet of mica.[3] Not even at night did his spirit-wife reappear. The lake, the land of the dead, had swallowed her up. As the sun rose above the mountains, the young man buried his face in his hands and wept.

Then he heard someone gently calling: "Hu-hu-hu," and felt the soft beating of wings on his back and shoulders. He looked up and saw an owl hovering above him. The owl said: "Young man, why are you weeping?"

He pointed to the lake, saying: "My beloved wife is down there in the land of the dead, where I cannot follow her."

"I know, poor man," said the owl. "Follow me to my house in the mountains, where I will tell you what to do. If you follow my advice, all will be well and you will be reunited with the one you love."

The owl led the husband to a cave in the mountains and, as they entered, the young man

---

3. **mica** (mī'kə): thin, flat, crystal-like mineral.

A Spirited Bunch

Traditionally, many American Indians have believed that the ghosts of the dead lived in a spirit land that was much like the land of the living, where the men hunted buffalo and the women tended to the children and home. The spirits sometimes left their realm and made contact with the living; the living could also make contact with the spirit world. As in this story, a mortal might seek out the soul of a departed loved one and travel to the bottom of a lake, across the galaxy, or over soaring mountains to locate the missing spirit. The reunion, if it occurred, was usually brief. It seems that the living and the dead do not make good long-term companions, and so each must finally return to his or her proper place.

found himself in a large room full of owl-men and owl-women. The owls greeted him warmly, inviting him to sit down and rest, to eat and drink. Gratefully he took his seat.

The old owl who had brought him took his owl clothing off, hanging it on an antler jutting out from the wall, and revealed himself as a manlike spirit. From a bundle in the wall this mysterious being took a small bag, showing it to the young man, telling him: "I will give this to you, but first I must instruct you in what you must do and must not do."

The young man eagerly stretched out his hand to grasp the medicine bag, but the owl drew back. "Foolish fellow, suffering from the impatience of youth! If you cannot curb your eagerness and your youthful desires, then even this medicine will be of no help to you."

"I promise to be patient," said the husband.

Of Feathers and Owls

In legends, birds and other natural objects often stand for abstract ideas. In this story, for example, feathers and owls play important roles.

- When the young man's wife appears as a floating red eagle plume, it's no accident. For the Zuni people the feather is a symbol of prayer and creativity. The eagle feather in particular represents honor—for example, the honor of a faithful, loving wife. And as for the color red, this fiery hue is often a symbol of love—but sometimes of death.

- The legend's other feathered friend, the owl, also carries special meaning. The Zuni believe that the departed spirits of wise elders and leaders disguise themselves as owls. With sharp eyes that see in the night and keen hunting skills, the owl might also serve as a wise and powerful nighttime guide.

"Well then," said the owl-man, "this is sleep medicine. It will make you fall into a deep sleep and transport you to some other place. When you awake, you will walk toward the Morning Star. Following the trail to the middle anthill, you will find your spirit-wife there. As the sun rises, so she will rise and smile at you, rise in the flesh, a spirit no more, and so you will live happily."

"But remember to be patient; remember to curb your eagerness. Let not your desire to touch and embrace her get the better of you, for if you touch her before bringing her safely home to the village of your birth, she will be lost to you forever."

Having finished this speech, the old owl-man blew some of the medicine on the young husband's face, who instantly fell into a deep sleep. Then all the strange owl-men put on their owl coats and, lifting the sleeper, flew with him to a place at the beginning of the trail to the middle anthill. There they laid him down underneath some trees.

Then the strange owl-beings flew on to the big lake at the bottom of which the land of the dead was located. The old owl-man's magic sleep medicine, and the feathered prayer sticks which the young man had carved, enabled them to dive down to the bottom of the lake and enter the land of the dead. Once inside, they used the sleep medicine to put to sleep the spirits who are in charge of that strange land beneath the waters. The owl-beings reverently laid their feathered prayer sticks before the altar of that netherworld, took up the beautiful young spirit-wife, and lifted her gently to the surface of the lake. Then, taking her upon their wings, they flew with her to the place where the young husband was sleeping.

When the husband awoke, he saw first the Morning Star, then the middle anthill, and then his wife at his side, still in deep slumber. Then she too awoke and opened her eyes

wide, at first not knowing where she was or what had happened to her. When she discovered her husband right by her side, she smiled at him, saying: "Truly, your love for me is strong, stronger than love has ever been, otherwise we would not be here."

They got up and began to walk toward the pueblo of their birth. The young man did not forget the advice the old owl-man had given him, especially the warning to not touch his wife until they had safely arrived at their home. In that way they traveled for four days, and all was well.

On the fourth day they arrived at Thunder Mountain and came to the river that flows by Salt Town. Then the young wife said: "My husband, I am very tired. The journey has been long and the days hot. Let me rest here awhile, let me sleep awhile, and then, refreshed, we can walk the last short distance home together." And her husband said: "We will do as you say."

The wife lay down and fell asleep. As her husband was watching over her, gazing at her loveliness, love so strong that he could not resist it overcame him, and he stretched out his hand and touched her.

She awoke instantly with a start, and, looking at him and at his hand upon her body, began to weep, the tears streaming down her face. At last she said: "You loved me, but you did not love me enough; otherwise you would have waited. Now I shall die again." And before his eyes her form faded and became transparent, and at the place where she had rested a few moments before, there was nothing. On a branch of a tree above him the old owl-man hooted mournfully: "Shame, shame, shame." Then the young man sank down in despair, burying his face in his hands, and ever after his mind wandered as his eyes stared vacantly.

If the young husband had controlled himself, if he had not longed to embrace his beautiful wife, if he had not touched her, if he had practiced patience and self-denial for only a short time, then death would have been overcome. There would be no journeying to the land below the lake, and no mourning for others lost.

But then, if there were no death, men would crowd each other with more people on this earth than the earth can hold. Then there would be hunger and war, with people fighting over a tiny patch of earth, over an ear of corn, over a scrap of meat. So maybe what happened was for the best.

Orpheus

A strikingly similar version of this legend appears in Greek mythology. There, the hero Orpheus (ôr'fē•əs), master of song, wooed and married the maiden Eurydice (yŏŏ•rid'i•sē'). When Eurydice died from a snakebite, the grieving Orpheus set off for the underworld to retrieve his beloved. Once there, he used his music and song to persuade Hades to release Eurydice. But the king of the underworld first set a condition: Under no circumstances was Orpheus or Eurydice to look back. The pair blissfully agreed and started on their way. Who can say why Orpheus did what he did next? He may have wanted to smile at his wife, or he may have begun to doubt that she was following him. Either way, in a moment of forgetfulness, Orpheus did the forbidden. He glanced back at Eurydice—only to see her instantly vanish. The grieving Orpheus spent his remaining days as a priest in the temple of Apollo, singing praise to the rational mind and condemning the foolish heart.

It is human to be paralyzed by grief, but it is heroic to be activated by it. The hero of this ancient Egyptian myth is a model of love, faithfulness, and above all, persistence. Follow the goddess Isis on her unusual quest to rescue her husband's body.

Isis the Queen

ROBERT D. SAN SOUCI

In the days when the gods were young and the sun was called the "Boat of Millions of Years," Osiris[1] ruled the land of Egypt. He was portrayed as a strong, handsome man with long, flowing hair that was as black as the fertile earth when wet by the life-giving waters of the Nile. His queen was Isis,[2] pictured as a beautiful woman dressed in robes of gold and green: gold for the sunrise, green for the crops she made grow. Together they ruled the land wisely, making it a place of peace and plenty.

But Osiris had a brother named Seth, who caused trouble wherever he went. Seth would take the shape of a strange-looking animal with red hair bristling like flame. Wherever he walked, the land turned brown and dry and the crops withered away.

Seth wanted to rule Egypt. When Osiris traveled to faraway places, leaving Isis to rule in his

You Need to Know...

- The great goddess of ancient Egypt was Isis, who was associated with the moon. Her husband, Osiris, was linked with the sun. Together they taught the first Egyptians how to make and follow laws and how to worship the gods. Isis taught mortals how to grind corn and how to use medicine. This queen, whose name literally means "throne," was thought to serve as the mother of each Egyptian king. It was believed that the throne itself transformed a man from prince into powerful ruler. Isis is often shown in paintings wearing a throne-shaped crown or the hieroglyph for the throne on her head.
- In ancient Egypt, burial rites could not be performed unless a person's body was whole. In turn, if burial rites were not performed, the person's spirit could not pass to Duat, the Land of the Dead.

---

1. **Osiris** (ō·sī'ris).
2. **Isis** (ī'sis).

absence, Seth tried to seize the throne, but Isis always prevented him from doing so. Each time, Osiris forgave his brother, and Isis, out of respect for her husband, did likewise.

Once, when Osiris returned from a long journey, Seth invited him to a banquet. Seth greeted Osiris warmly and invited him to feast on rare food and drink from all over the known world.

After the meal, Seth announced, "I have a gift for someone here." Drawing back a curtain, he revealed a cedar chest shaped like a man and inlaid with ebony[3] and ivory. All of the guests marveled at the craftsmanship.

"This belongs to the person who fits inside perfectly," Seth told them.

One by one, his guests stretched out inside the chest. But each was too thin or fat, too tall or short. Finally, Seth said to Osiris, "My brother, you are the only one who has not tried."

Osiris stepped in and lay down with his arms at his sides. The contours of the chest fit him perfectly. Instantly, Seth slammed the cover shut, then had it nailed and sealed with molten lead. He then set the chest adrift on the Nile. The current carried it swiftly downstream toward the "Great Green" (Mediterranean Sea). Osiris suffocated to death in the chest, which became his coffin.

When Isis discovered Seth's treachery, she raced to the river's edge searching frantically for her husband. As she continued her lengthy search along the riverbank, Seth claimed the throne of Egypt.

▲ Isis, the Great Goddess.

---

3. **ebony** (eb'ə•nē): dark wood used in furniture.

Where the Nile flowed into the Great Green, Isis met some children playing on the shore. She asked one boy, "Have you seen a chest of cedar inlaid with ebony and ivory and shaped like a man?"

"Yes, my lady," the child answered. "I saw it carried eastward by the waves. I watched until I could see it no longer."

Isis followed the shore eastward until she came to the ancient city of Byblos (in Lebanon). There she used her magic arts to learn that, during her years of searching, a huge tamarisk tree had grown around Osiris's coffin. This tree was now a pillar in the main hall of the king's palace.

At her request, the king of Byblos had the pillar cut down and opened. Isis pulled out the chest, wept over the body of her husband, and put the coffin into a boat. She sailed back to Egypt, grieving for her lost love.

Isis hid her husband's body in a thicket of papyrus.[4] One day while Seth was out hunting, he found Osiris's body and

---

4. **papyrus** (pə•pī′rəs): tall plant that grows along the banks of rivers.

Book of the Dead written in Egyptian hieroglyphics. ▶

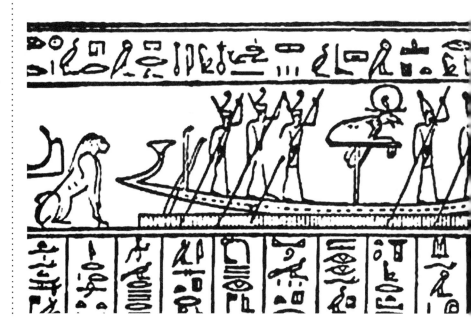

cut it into fourteen pieces. He scattered these pieces throughout Egypt, but Isis searched until she recovered thirteen of
them. She then vowed that she would give Osiris a son to
avenge his death and reclaim his throne.

Using the most powerful magic she could devise, Isis drew
into herself a part of the fourteenth piece, which she was
unable to locate. This was the spirit of Osiris, which entered
her as air and light. She felt new life in herself as the child of
Osiris grew beneath her heart.

By heaven's power, Osiris became god of the dead. All
Egyptians who died had to pass before him and prove them-
selves sinless before they could go on to Iaru, the "Field of
Reeds," on the eastern horizon.

Isis was left on earth to raise her son, whom she named
Horus and whose sign was the falcon. In time, Horus defeated Seth in a series of contests, and the gods decided to allow
him to ascend to the throne. Ever after, the pharaohs and

queens of Egypt held the falcon in high esteem and forbade their subjects to harm this bird.

Seth remained the "Red God" of the desert, whose power was felt in every windstorm that whipped the desert sands. Isis was honored as the "Thousand Named Goddess," but the Egyptians most often called her simply "Isis the Queen." In time, worship of this popular goddess spread throughout the ancient Greek and Roman world.

Enter the World of the Dead

The ancient Egyptians believed that to be admitted to the Land of the Dead, a person's body had to be preserved. (To preserve something is to keep it from decaying.) They also believed that a body had to be reunited with its spirit, which had fled the body at death. To preserve the body and to lure back its spirit, the ancient Egyptians developed a practice known as embalming. There were several methods of embalming a corpse. If the corpse was royalty, the brain, intestines, and other organs were removed, washed, and stored in beautiful jars filled with herbs. Powders and perfumes were placed in the body, which was then immersed in a salty bath for ten weeks. After that, the body was washed, wrapped in cotton strips, covered in a resin, placed in a coffin, and buried in a tomb. Simpler methods were used for common people. These sometimes included the injection of oils before the salt bath or sometimes, for the very poor, nothing but the salt bath and purging of the intestines.

Problem solving is a team effort. Even when you feel as if you are solving a problem alone, there are many invisible helpers at work—for example, those who have taught you how to think and those who will help you put your plan into action. As you read this African dilemma tale, consider the actions of each character. Which helper, if any, is the biggest hero?

The Five Helpers

RETOLD BY A.W. CARDINALL

There was once a beautiful girl, the daughter of a chief. She was finer to look upon than any other girl that men could see. But there was no one whom she would agree to marry.

Men came from all countries, but she would not have them. And all the land heard the news of this girl, that though she was of marriageable age, she would take no one.

There was also a snake, a large python who dwelt in a vast lake nearby the river. When he heard about this girl, he decided that he would marry her. So he changed himself into a man and came to the village.

As soon as the maiden saw the young man she was delighted, and said she would marry him at once. Everyone was pleased, and that night they took the young man and the girl on to the roof of the house, for the houses in that village had flat roofs, and there they left them.

Now during the night, the snake licked the girl all over and

> **You Need to Know...**
> A dilemma tale is a story that ends with a question that asks the listeners to choose among several alternatives. By encouraging animated discussion, a dilemma tale invites its audience to think about right and wrong behavior and about how to best live within society. Dilemma tales are like folk tales in that they are usually short, simple, and driven entirely by plot. As you read this tale, keep in mind that most African cultures were traditionally oral ones. That is, their stories and tales are meant to be told aloud.

swallowed her, and changing again into his snake form, he made off to the great lake.

Next morning people came to the house and called to the girl and her man to come down. There was no answer, and the chief told the people to climb up and see what was the matter. This they did, and reported that both the girl and the man were missing.

The chief was very angry, and at once ordered all the people to follow the girl and her lover. But they could find no tracks. So they called for a man who could smell everything. He at once smelled the trail of the girl and followed it down to the great water. There he could go no further. The people, urged on by the anger of the chief, then called on a man famous through all the country for his thirst. They told him to drink up the lake. This he did. But still there was no sign of the man or the girl. Then the people called a man famous for his capacity for work and told him to take out all the mud from the lake. This he did, and thereby revealed a hole. But it was so deep that no one could reach the bottom. Then they remembered that there was a man with an arm that could stretch over all the Dagomba Island. They told him to put his arm in the hole and pull. Out came the great python, which was immediately killed. And when they had cut open its stomach, they found the girl inside, but she was dead. Then the people remembered a man who had the power of medicine, and was able to raise the dead. He came at once and restored the girl to life. Now which of those five men did best?

Some birthday cakes have trick candles that flare back to life after they've been blown out. And some of our most beloved heroes act the same way. Time and again, in the face of extinction they find a way to stay alive. Now meet Sindbad the Sailor, a hero whose big ideas (along with a healthy dose of luck) keep him ever hopeful in the face of hopelessness.

ARABIAN FOLK TALE

The Third Voyage of Sindbad

RETOLD BY ANDREW LANG

Turning away from the sea we wandered miserably inland, finding as we went various herbs and fruits which we ate, feeling that we might as well live as long as possible though we had no hope of escape. Presently we saw in the far distance what seemed to be a splendid palace, toward which we turned our weary steps, but when we reached it we saw that it was a castle, lofty and strongly built. Pushing back the heavy ebony doors we entered the courtyard, but upon the threshold of the great hall beyond it we paused, frozen with horror, at the sight which greeted us. On one side lay a huge pile of bones— human bones, and on the other numberless spits[1] for roasting!

Overcome with despair we sank trembling to the ground

> **You Need to Know...**
> The speaker in this story is an adventurer known as Sindbad the Sailor. In a collection of stories called *The Thousand and One Nights*, Sindbad describes his seven voyages to distant lands. (You can read more about *The Thousand and One Nights* on page 125.) Having carelessly spent his fortune, the young Sindbad sets sail from Baghdad. His plan is to recover his lost wealth through trade in the Far East. However, his voyages are far from easy. Time and again, Sindbad and his crew are lost, shipwrecked, starved, and driven to despair. A cast of frightful, fantastical creatures makes matters worse. Among these are a swarm of apes, a man-eating serpent, and a gigantic, stone-dropping bird—not to mention the hulking host of the castle that you are about to enter.

---

1. spits: rods on which meat is cooked over a fire.

and lay there without speech or motion. The sun was setting when a loud noise aroused us, the door of the hall was violently burst open and a horrible giant entered. He was as tall as a palm tree, perfectly black, and had but one eye, which flamed like a burning coal in the middle of his forehead. His teeth were long and sharp and he grinned horribly, while his lower lip hung down upon his chest, and he had ears like elephant's ears, which covered his shoulders, and nails like the claws of some fierce bird.

The sun was setting when a loud noise aroused us, the door of the hall was violently burst open and a horrible giant entered.

At this terrible sight our senses left us and we lay like dead men. When at last we came to ourselves the giant sat examining us attentively with his fearful eye. Presently, when he had looked at us enough, he came toward us and, stretching out his hand, took me by the back of the neck, turning me this way and that, but feeling that I was mere skin and bone he set me down again and went on to the next, whom he treated in the same fashion. At last he came to the captain, and finding him the fattest of us all, he took him up in one hand and stuck him upon a spit and proceeded to kindle a huge fire at which he presently roasted him. After the giant had supped[2] he lay down to sleep, snoring like the loudest thunder, while we lay shivering with horror the whole night through. When day broke the giant awoke and went out, leaving us in the castle.

---

2. **supped:** ate the meal usually eaten in the evening.

When we believed him to be really gone we started up, bemoaning our horrible fate until the hall echoed with our despairing cries. Though we were many and our enemy was alone it did not occur to us to kill him. Indeed we should have found that a hard task even if we had thought of it, but no plan could we devise to deliver ourselves. So at last, submitting to our sad fate, we spent the day in wandering up and down the island, eating such fruits as we could find, and when night came we returned to the castle, having sought in vain for any other place of shelter.

At sunset the giant returned, supped upon one of our unhappy comrades, slept and snored till dawn, and then left us as before. Our condition seemed to us so frightful that several of my companions thought it would be better to leap from the cliffs and perish in the waves at once, rather than await so miserable an end; but I had a plan of escape which I now unfolded to them, and which they at once agreed to attempt.

"Listen, my brothers," I said, "you know that plenty of driftwood lies along the shore. Let us make several rafts and carry them to a suitable place. If our plot succeeds, we can wait patiently for the chance of some passing ship which would rescue us from this fatal island. If it fails, we must quickly take to our rafts; frail as they are, we have more chance of saving our lives with them than we have if we remain here."

Hero in a Frame

The origin of *The Thousand and One Nights,* also known as *The Arabian Nights,* is a mystery. No one is sure where the collection came from or who first put it together. Some scholars believe that it grew out of stories from India and China or Central Asia. A fantastical hodgepodge, *The Thousand and One Nights* includes tales about Sindbad, Aladdin and his lamp, and Ali Baba and the forty thieves. A larger story, known as a **frame story,** holds it all together. In this frame story, an angry king kills his wife for being unfaithful and then marries and kills a different wife each day. Finally, a woman named Scheherazade (shə•her'ə•zäd') marries the king and begins telling him a different fascinating story every night. However, she leaves each story unfinished, promising to tell the ending the next night. The king, enchanted by the tales, puts off her death, and after one thousand and one nights, he allows her to live.

All agreed with me, and we spent the day in building rafts, each capable of carrying three persons. At nightfall we returned to the castle, and very soon in came the giant and one more of our number was sacrificed. But the time of our vengeance was at hand! As soon as he had finished his horrible repast he lay down to sleep as before, and when we heard him begin to snore I, and nine of the boldest of my comrades, rose softly and each took a spit, which we made red-hot in the fire, and then at a given signal we plunged it with one accord into the giant's eye, completely blinding him. Uttering a terrible cry, he sprang to his feet clutching in all directions to try to seize one of us, but we had all fled different ways as soon as the deed was done and thrown ourselves flat upon the ground in corners where he was not likely to touch us with his feet.

After a vain search he fumbled about till he found the door and fled out of it, howling frightfully. As for us, when he was gone we made haste to leave the fatal castle and, stationing ourselves beside our rafts, we waited to see what would happen.

Our idea was that if, when the sun rose, we saw nothing of the giant and no longer heard his howls, which still came faintly through the darkness, growing more and more distant, we should conclude that he was dead and that we might safely stay upon the island and need not risk our lives upon the frail rafts. But alas! morning light showed us our enemy approaching, supported on either hand by two giants nearly as large and fearful as himself, while a crowd of others followed close upon their heels. Hesitating no longer we clambered upon our rafts and rowed with all our might out to sea.

The giants, seeing their prey escaping them, seized huge pieces of rock and, wading into the water, hurled them after us with such good aim that all the rafts except the one I was on were swamped and their luckless crews drowned, without our being able to do anything to help them. Indeed I and my two companions had all we could do to keep our own raft beyond the reach of the giants, but by dint of hard rowing we at last gained the open sea. Here we were at the mercy of the winds and waves, which tossed us to and fro all that day and night, but the next morning we found ourselves near an island, upon which we gladly landed.

The giants hurled rocks at the rafts. ▶

Connections — GRECO-ROMAN EPIC

Several of Sindbad's adventures mirror those of other heroes. For example, a giant with one eye also appears in the Greek epic poem the *Odyssey*. Wearied by the Trojan War, the hero Ulysses seeks merely to return to his home. However, trap after trap is laid in Ulysses' path. Read on to see this hero in action—and to meet yet another man-eating menace.

Ulysses and the Cyclops

RETOLD BY Alfred J. Church

All day Ulysses[1] thought how he might save himself and his companions, and the end of his thinking was this. There was a great pole in the cave, the trunk of an olive tree, green wood which the giant was going to use as a staff for walking when it should have been dried by the

---

1. **Ulysses** (yŏŏ•lis'ēz').

smoke. Ulysses cut off this a piece some six feet long, and his companions hardened it in the fire, and hid it away. In the evening the giant came back and did as before, seizing two of the prisoners and devouring them. When he had finished his meal, Ulysses came to him with the skin[2] of wine in his hand and said, "Drink, Cyclops,[3] now that you have supped. Drink this wine, and see what good things we had on our ship. But no one will bring the like to you in your island here if you are so cruel to strangers."

The Cyclops took the skin and drank, and was mightily pleased with the wine.

"Give me more," he said, "and tell me your name, and I will give you a gift such as a host should. Truly this is a fine drink, like, I take it, to that which the gods have in heaven."

Then Ulysses said, "My name is No Man. And now give me your gift."

"And the giant said, "My gift is this: you shall be eaten last." And as he said this, he fell back in a drunken sleep.

Then Ulysses said to his companions, "Be brave, my friends, for the time is come for us to be delivered from this prison."

So they put the stake into the fire, and kept it there till it was ready, green as it was, to burst into flame. Then they thrust it into his eye, for, as has been told, he had but one, and Ulysses leaned with all his force upon the stake, and turned it about, just as a man turns a drill about when he would make a hole in a ship timber. And the wood hissed in the eye as the red-hot iron hisses in the water when a smith would temper it to make a sword.

Then the giant leaped up, and tore away the stake, and cried out so loudly that the round-eyed people in the island came to see what had happened.

---

2. **skin:** container for liquids made from an animal's skin.

3. **Cyclops** (sī'kläps'): giant with one eye in the middle of its forehead.

◀ They thrust the stake into the giant's eye.

"What ails you," they asked, "that you make so great an uproar, waking us all out of our sleep? Is anyone stealing your sheep or seeking to hurt you?"

And the giant bellowed, "No Man is hurting me."

"Well," said the round-eyed people, "if no man is hurting you, then it must be the gods that do it, and we cannot help you against them."

But Ulysses laughed when he thought how he had beguiled[4] them by his name. But he was still in doubt how he and his companions should escape, for the giant sat in the mouth of the cave, and felt to see whether the men were trying to get out among the sheep. And Ulysses, after long thinking, made a plan by which he and his companions might escape. By great good luck the giant had driven the rams into the cave, for he commonly left them outside. These rams were very big and strong, and Ulysses took six of the biggest, and tied the six men that were left out of the twelve underneath their bellies with osier[5] twigs. And on each side of the six rams to which a

---

4. **beguiled** (bē•gīld'): tricked.
5. **osier** (o'zhər): willow.

man was tied, he put another ram. So he himself was left, for there was no one who could do the same for him. Yet this also he managed. There was a very big ram, much bigger than all the others, and to this he clung, grasping the fleece with both his hands. So, when the morning came, the flocks went out of the cave as they were used to doing, and the giant felt them as they passed by him, and did not perceive the men. And when he felt the biggest ram, he said,

"How is this? You are not used to lag behind; you are always the first to run to the pasture in the morning and to come back to the fold at night. Perhaps you are troubled about thy master's eye which this villain No Man has destroyed. First he overcame me with wine, and then he put out my eye. Oh! that you could speak and tell me where he is! I would dash out his brains upon the ground." And then he let the big ram go.

When they were out of the giant's reach, Ulysses let go his hold of the ram, and loosed his companions, and they all made as much haste as they could to get to the place where they had left their ship, looking back to see whether the giant was following them. The crew at the ship were very glad to see them. . . .

Read On

If you find Scheherazade's predicament fascinating, you might enjoy *Scheherazade's Cat* by Amy Zerner (Zerner/Farber), a collection of fables about a cat that saves the life of her mistress. More adventures of Sindbad and Odysseus (Ulysses) are found in *Sindbad: From the Tales of the Thousand and One Nights* retold by Ludmila Zeman (Tundra) and *The Wanderings of Odysseus: The Story of the Odyssey* by Rosemary Sutcliff (Delacorte).

CHAPTER 4
Transformations

The More They Change . . .

Stories of transformation appeal to our desire to change the way things are. Some of these stories are about the transformation of a person into another form—an animal, an insect, or a stone. Other tales of metamorphosis are about the way that a person's character changes.

Now for a look at some of our most popular shape-changers. These guys (and others like them) give us an up-close look at one of the world's oldest paradoxes—how both good and evil can lurk within the heart of a single human being.

The **werewolf** cannot resist a full moon—even if he's unwilling to be transformed. The werewolf legend originated in Germany, a heavily wooded country where wolves were a constant threat. People in Russia thought some people turned into snakes; in India, tigers; and in the China, bullfrogs.

Vampires are thought to be the restless souls of dead people. Vampires return to life at night and wander the earth—sometimes in the form of a bat or even a wolf—searching for human blood. Keep a mirror or a flashlight handy: If the suspect does not have a reflection or a shadow—well, run for the garlic!

One of the original "evil twins," Mr. Hyde was born in 1886 when Robert Louis Stevenson published his novel *The Strange Case of Dr. Jekyll and Mr. Hyde*. In this fascinating tale, a medical doctor becomes convinced

▲ Dr. Jekyll is transformed into Mr. Hyde.

INVESTIGATE:

Can you think of other common creatures that can change their appearance in some way?

that he can separate his good personality from his bad one—and thereby control the latter. Unfortunately, the good guy loses the upper hand.

It's Only Natural

You may think that shape-changers live only in the world of the imagination. Actually, they can be found just about anywhere.

• **Color-changers.** Okay, so they do not actually change shape. However, would you not feel like a different creature if you changed from brown to green? Animals who change colors usually do so for protection. For example, a hungry fox is less likely to see a green lizard on a green leaf than on a brown one. Likewise, the hare whose fur turns white in winter gets instant concealment— snow!

• **Form-changers.** *Caterpillar* literally means "hairy cat." Although these creepy-crawlers do not really turn into cats, they do change into other creatures—butterflies and moths. Like Superman in a phone booth, the cater-pillar goes into its cocoon with one form and comes out with an entirely different one. In nature, total transformations such as this are known as *metamorphoses.*

• **Animals with cloaking devices.** Some animals have color schemes involving spots, stripes, or other pat-terns. These patterns help the animal blend into its background so that when it moves toward its prey, it goes undetected. For example, a cheetah's spots are hard to see against a scrubby landscape, and some snakes' long green stripes weave and wave just like the surrounding blades of grass.

Many love-struck people claim to have been pierced by Cupid's arrow. However, what happens when Cupid himself enters someone's heart? Read the following ancient Greek myth to find out.

Cupid and Psyche

RETOLD BY IDRIES SHAH

Once upon a time there was a great King, who had three fair daughters. And they were so beautiful that from many lands suitors came to seek their hands in marriage.

The youngest was the loveliest of all, so that people said that she was like the goddess Aphrodite,[1] and they bowed low as she passed through the streets of the city.

Now it was not long since Paris[2] had given the goddess Aphrodite the apple for being the fairest of all the goddesses, and she was jealous. She summoned her son, Cupid, and said to him, "Come, let us fly together to see this mortal maiden whom men say is the image of me." They reached the palace where Psyche[3] was sleeping, and when his mother showed the girl to him, she said to him: "Prick her with one of the arrows of love

> **You Need to Know...**
> Cupid is the name the Romans gave to the Greek god Eros, the god of love. In early stories, Cupid appears as a lovely but serious youth, often a bearer of gifts. In later stories, he becomes the chubby bow-and-arrow boy that we still know today. This mischievous marksman flies about, shooting arrows of love into the hearts of gods and humans alike. He sometimes uses his skill in the service of his mother Aphrodite's jealous whims. More often than not, though, his shots are random, playful, and unpredictable. For this reason, Cupid is often shown wearing a blindfold. Love is blind, after all, and can strike anyone, anywhere, at any time.

---

1. **Aphrodite** (afˈrə•dītˈē): Greek goddess of love and beauty.
2. **Paris:** son of Priam, king of Troy, who was asked to judge which of three goddesses—Aphrodite, Hera, or Pallas Athene—was the most beautiful.
3. **Psyche** (sīˈkē).

so that she will feel the deepest affection for one of the basest of mortal men. Avenge me, my son." Then she departed.

Cupid, however, gazing upon the girl, was stricken with pity and said "I will never do you so much wrong as to mate you with some wretch not good enough for you. You are safe from my darts." And he flew away.

Now, though all men bowed down before Psyche, none dared marry her, for she seemed too good and pure. So while her sisters married, and had husbands whom they loved, Psyche remained untouched and unsought. When she had reached the age when Greek maidens should be wed, the King grew anxious, and went to consult the oracle. When he returned, with ashen face, his Queen asked him what had been the oracle's answer. "Psyche must be left on a desolate mountainside until some monster comes to devour her," said the King. "Men have paid her honors only reserved for the gods, and the gods require vengeance."

The Queen and her maidens wept and wailed, but Psyche remained calm. At last a white-clad priest came to tell the King he must tarry no longer. Soon a procession, each person clad in black, left the city, Psyche led by her father and mother, and singers sang a mournful dirge. The sun was rising when they reached a bare rock; and here it was that the oracle had directed Psyche should be left to perish.

When for the last time her parents took her in their arms, Psyche never shed a tear in farewell. After all, what good was it to mourn, when it was surely all the will of the gods?

Not daring to look back, in case they should see the dreadful monster actually devouring their daughter, the King and Queen went away with their retainers. Psyche was very tired, for she had walked a long way, so she leaned wearily against the rock. Soon a deep sleep came over her, and her sorrows were forgotten.

▲ *Cupid and Psyche* by John Roddam Spencer Stanhope.

While she slept, Cupid was looking down at her, and at his bidding Zephyr[4] lifted her up gently and carried her away to lay her down upon a bed of lilies in the valley.

While she slept, beautiful dreams wafted[5] through her mind. She woke feeling happy, she did not know why, and, getting to her feet, began to walk toward a beautiful palace made of ivory and gold. A little timidly, she stepped into the palace, and passed from room to room without coming to the end of the wonders there. Out of the silence a voice said in her ear: "Everything you see is yours, so enjoy the palace

---

4. **Zephyr** (zef'ər): gentle breeze named for the ancient Greek god of the west wind, Zephyrus.

5. **wafted** (wäft'id): carried, as on a breeze.

and its contents as if it were your own home." There was a table set with every delicacy, forks and spoons of gold, and unseen fingers played music upon the harp.

When evening came, a great calm came upon Psyche, and she heard someone say "Place this veil upon your head, for you are to be a bride," and a golden veil descended upon her, covering her face. Then a cake was put into her hand, and the same voice said "Eat half of this cake and I will eat the other half." She did so with trembling fingers, and she

---

She heard the voice again, "You are now my wife, and you will live in this palace with me as long as you live."

---

saw that the rest of the cake had vanished. "Now listen to what I say," she heard the voice again, "You are now my wife, and you will live in this palace with me as long as you live. But, one word of warning: your sisters may find you here, and if they come, do not tell them anything about this ceremony, for their love can turn to hate very quickly, out of jealousy."

Psyche nodded, and promised that she would do as her unseen husband decreed.[6] But after a few weeks of bliss she began to feel unhappy at being without friends of her own age, and sometimes cried beside the fountain. One evening she felt her husband's fingers stroking her hair, asking, "What makes you so unhappy, my dear?" "It is because I miss my sisters and my friends," she answered, and continued, "Could I not see my sisters even for a little while? After

---

6. **decreed:** officially ordered.

◀ Castle of Beauty and the Beast.

Beauty's Family

The story of Cupid and Psyche was lost and forgotten during most of the Middle Ages. However, in the 1400s, the story reappeared in Europe and was gradually translated into many languages. Each version took on the color, landscape, and folklore of its local culture. The result was a family of stories known as the Beauty and the Beast tales. If you are familiar with the story of Beauty and the Beast, you may spy certain similarities between it and the Cupid-Psyche story. Both feature a young maiden who is sacrificed to a husband whose true beauty is hidden, and a set of jealous sisters. However, the stories have obvious differences. Beauty's father is a merchant rather than a king, and the family's misfortune does not come from a jealous goddess but from the loss of their wealth. Beauty learns to love Beast in spite of his ugliness, while Psyche fears her husband's true form. The stories are linked, though, in their basic message: True love sees beyond the surface.

all, I have not been devoured by any monster, they might like to know what has happened to me." There was silence for a few moments; then the voice said "I am afraid that ill[7] may come of your wish, but if you remember what I told you and do not tell them everything, I am happy for you to invite your sisters here." Psyche was overjoyed, and promised to tell them nothing.

"Then, tomorrow," said he, "I shall tell my servant, Zephyr, to carry them here." And next morning Zephyr found her sisters seated on the rock, beating their breasts and crying. Suddenly, they found themselves wafted gently to the palace where Psyche was sitting. Soon they were laughing together, and the great table was groaning[8] with food and silver, and they ate till they could eat no more.

"Now, tell us what happened to you after you were left on that dreadful rock" asked the eldest sister; and the other inquired "Where is your husband? and *who* is he?" Their growing suspicion boded[9] no good for Psyche, and she began to be afraid for her secret. "Oh, he goes out hunting a lot," she said, "I would like you to come into the treasure-room with me and choose some presents." The sight of so much gold and so many jewels and precious objects turned their heads completely. The gifts they were given were of immense value, and when Zephyr bore[10] the girls away, unknown to them, Psyche felt that she did not want to see her sisters again for quite some time.

"You told them nothing, I hope?" asked her husband that night, "For they could be plotting your downfall, you know . . ."

---

7. **ill:** something bad or harmful.

8. **groaning:** loaded down.

9. **boded:** predicted; foretold.

10. **bore:** carried.

"No, I remembered what you said, husband, and indeed I was glad to see them go, for they have become very jealous of me," said Psyche.

"Good," said he, sighing, "for the present moment all seems well, but be careful that you do not let them know the true state of affairs, or much ill fortune will come to us."

"I promise you," said Psyche, "I will never tell them. Let them come again, and I will show you how I can be silent!"

So the sisters came again, Psyche wanting to show her husband that he could trust her completely.

At first the other two girls behaved as if they were glad of their sister's good fortune, then one said "Oh, dearest sister, I've been so worried about you and the dreadful thing which had happened to you that I can scarcely speak."

"Why, what do you mean?" asked Psyche, trembling. Her blood ran cold when she saw the look on their faces. "Tell me, and do not beat about the bush. What is it?"

"Your husband, dear sister, who is he? Where is he from? From where does he get all this treasure? My dear, believe us, we are only thinking of your own good . . ." and the two sisters began to wring their hands.

Psyche shook her elder sister's arm and said: "Tell me, what have you heard about my husband?"

"We have it on the very best authority," said her sister, "that your husband is not as you think, but a huge and poisonous snake which is full of venom. People working in the fields have seen it swimming across

▲ Psyche sneaking a look at her sleeping husband's face.

the river. Believe us, we would not like to tell you this, but . . ."

Psyche recoiled[11] with horror. "It is true I have never yet seen my husband's face," she cried, "He warned me that if ever I were to look upon him he would be forced to abandon me forever. And yet, and yet, he is always so gentle to me."

"We have something here to help you see his true form," the sisters chorused, placing a small oil-lamp into Psyche's hand, "Tonight, when he is asleep, light this and look upon that dreadful face. Then you can happily return with us and be free of him!"

They both embraced her, and were wafted home on the wings of Zephyr.

Left alone, Psyche wept, and for hours tried to subdue[12] her misery. When at last her husband came in, she managed to hide her deceit. So well did she feign[13] happiness that he did not suspect anything was wrong as she welcomed him. Soon he was asleep by her side. For a few moments Psyche wondered whether she dare light the lamp or not, then she felt she had to know. She leaned over the bed and held the flame close to him. Instead of the dreadful

---

11. recoiled (ri•koild'): pulled back from.

12. subdue (səb•dōō'): to overcome.

13. feign (fān): pretend.

monster she had expected there was the most beautiful of all the gods, Cupid himself.

At this sight Psyche started[14] and a drop of burning oil fell on Cupid's shoulder. He woke, and looked at her reproachfully. He turned, and would have flown away, but Psyche grasped his leg, and was borne up with him into the air, till she fell to the ground and fainted away.

Then, after she had regained consciousness, she spent a long time searching and calling for her husband, weeping and begging him to return. Wandering through the country, one day she came to a temple, where she saw sheaves of oats, ears of corn, and scythes[15] all scattered in wild confusion. Attempting to bring some order to the chaos, she began to tidy the place; and then she heard a loud voice from afar: "Unhappy girl! You have brought down the

---

14. **started:** moved suddenly.

15. **scythes** (si*th*z): tools with a curved blade fixed on a long handle, used for cutting grass and grains.

Valentine V.I.P.

Legend has it that Valentine's Day began with a priest in third-century Rome. The emperor wanted to make sure his soldiers thought only about war, and so he outlawed marriage for young men. According to legend, Valentine sympathized with the young men and began performing secret marriages. The cost of Valentine's defiance was his life, and the reward was sainthood.

Cupid has costarred in this romantic holiday since the 1400s, when he appeared on a valentine card showing a lady, her knight, and Cupid aiming an arrow at the knight's heart. Cupid remains one of the popular symbols of love and continues to appear on valentine cards today.

wrath of the goddess Aphrodite on your head. Go, leave this temple in case you also draw down on me the fury of the goddess."

Not knowing where her feet would lead her, Psyche wandered on, still searching and crying. At last she was tracked down by one of Aphrodite's servants, who took her to the sacred presence of the goddess herself. Here she was whipped and beaten, and was made to separate a large heap of seeds of all kinds—wheat, millet, barley. The task seemed to be hopeless, but Aphrodite left her to do it, under strict instructions from the goddess to put each of them in an individual pile. As she sat and wept, a tiny ant came, and seeing her plight,[16] brought all his brothers, and by nightfall every

---

16. **plight** (plīt): unhappy and difficult situation.

▲ Sculpture of Aphrodite from around 350 B.C.

From the Head or the Heart?

- *Psyche* is the Greek word for "soul." In the English language, it is associated with another invisible part of the human being—the mind. *Psychology*, then, is the study of the mind, and a *psychiatrist* is a doctor who treats mental conditions.
- Aphrodite was the mother of Cupid, but her Roman counterpart, Venus, gave birth to more English words. For example, the words *winsome* (meaning "charming") and *venerate* (meaning "to honor") both derive from Venus's name. These words show some aspects of the goddess's character. However, there is another side to her. For instance, a person who is *vain* is overly conceited, and a snake that is *venomous* is poisonous. (The word *venom* comes from the Latin word *venenum*—the love potion on Cupid's darts.) *Venus*, of course, is also the name of the brightest planet in our sky—and the only planet in our solar system named after a goddess.

grain was sorted and in its own bag. Psyche waited, trembling with fear, for Aphrodite to enter the room.

When she did enter, Aphrodite was seized with anger and cried: "Wretched girl! It is not through your own labor that this has been done! Now, in yonder glade,[17] there are some sheep whose coats are as bright as gold and as soft as silk. Tomorrow morning at dawn I want you to go out there, shear them, and bring in enough wool to make me a robe. And this time I do not think you will have any help!" So saying, she disappeared.

Next day, very early, Psyche went out to the glade, and looked into the clear waters of the river. A reed sang to her: "O Psyche, fear nothing. The sheep must be shorn at evening, for during the day you will not be able to catch them. When they lie exhausted, you can gather all the wool you need from the branches of the shrubs and the hedges through which they have been rushing wildly all day."

So Psyche did as the reed told her, and waited till the cool of the evening, and gathered enough wool for the goddess. But when she gave it to Aphrodite, she was greeted with scowls of rage and ordered to go to the top of a lofty mountain to fill an urn[18] from a fountain of black water. The urn was of the finest crystal, and Psyche carried it up most carefully in case she should drop it. But when she got there she found the fountain was guarded by two terrible dragons. She would have started back without the water, had not a giant eagle taken the vessel from her hand and filled it, telling the dragons that Aphrodite needed the precious water to add fresh luster to her beauty.

---

17. **glade** (glād): open, grassy space in a wood or forest.

18. **urn** (urn): vase.

▲ Cupid pleading with the gods on Mount Olympus.

Joyfully the eagle brought Psyche the precious urn filled with the black water, and she gave it to the goddess. But still Aphrodite was not satisfied. Each time she was given new tasks and errands, birds and beasts helped her, and the goddess was quite frustrated in her desire to destroy Psyche.

If Cupid had only known that Psyche was suffering so many privations,[19] he would have somehow contrived to save her, but the wound where the boiling oil had fallen took a long time to heal. At last, when it was completely healed, he visited Psyche, and she was overjoyed at the sound of his voice. She poured out all the story of her sufferings, and Cupid was grieved for her. He said "Your punishment has been more than a mortal ought to be asked to endure, and though I am not able to save you from my mother's wrath, I will fly to Mount Olympus, and beseech the gods to grant you forgiveness."

And so he did. In the fullness of time Psyche was rescued from her trials on Earth, and left the world of humans, to sit among the immortals on Mount Olympus, forever immortal herself.

19. **privations** (prī•vā'shənz): hardships.

At the end of "Cupid and Psyche," Psyche becomes immortal. Like the butterfly, she has been transformed from an earth-crawler to a creature of the sky. For this reason, Psyche is often shown with butterfly wings. Such dramatic changes are not only the stuff of myths. All things in nature—including you—are constantly growing and changing. Here, an ancient Chinese philosopher comments on this idea in the form of an anecdote, or brief story.

The Butterfly

Chuang Tzu

TRANSLATED BY Moss Roberts

Chuang Tzu said, "Once upon a time I dreamed myself a butterfly, floating like petals in the air, happy to be doing as I pleased, no longer aware of myself! But soon enough I awoke and then, frantically clutching myself, Chuang Tzu I was! I wonder: Was Chuang Tzu dreaming himself the butterfly, or was the butterfly dreaming itself Chuang Tzu? Of course, if you take Chuang Tzu and the butterfly together, then there's a difference between them. But that difference is only due to their changing material forms."

Have you ever challenged someone to a contest and then later regretted it? In retrospect, it is always easy to see when we have been too sure of ourselves. However, the experience of losing a contest—even though it hurts—can sometimes bring about transformation. Read this ancient Greek myth for a vivid example.

Pallas Athene and Arachne

AMY CRUSE

Pallas Athene was, next to Hera, the greatest among the ancient Greek goddesses. She was the goddess of wisdom, and she watched over everything that had to do with the safety and prosperity of the state. She loved peace, but she helped the people to fight when their country was attacked; and though she bore no weapons, she went armored in helmet and breastplate, and over her shoulders hung a goatskin to which was fastened a broad and shining shield. This was the aegis, and any person over whom it was cast was safe from all hurt or danger. Athene also taught the people many useful arts—how to till[1] the ground and rear[2] cattle. She invented the rake and the plow, and the bridle by means of which the people might tame the wild horses to their service. To the women she taught the

You Need to Know...

Hidden within this myth is a smaller one that mirrors the first—like a photograph of a person taking a photograph. In this case, both stories feature a mortal who is overpowered by a god. The smaller myth concerns the almighty Zeus and a mortal named Europa. Europa awakes one morning after a troubling dream in which two continents try to claim her as their own. Fleeing the dream, she goes with her companions to gather flowers by the sea. Meanwhile, Aphrodite shoots an arrow into the heart of Zeus, and the great god falls instantly in love with the lovely maiden. He transforms himself into a handsome bull and appears to Europa, who is drawn to him like a magnet. Climbing onto his back, Europa finds herself swept away over the great ocean to Zeus's island home of Crete. There, she becomes his bride—and later the namesake of her own continent, Europe.

---

1. **till:** to plow land and raise crops.
2. **rear:** to raise; help to grow up.

arts of spinning, weaving, embroidering, and all kinds of needlework; so that as time went on the women of Greece became famed for the beautiful work that they produced.

There was one maiden, named Arachne, whose skill was greater than that of any other woman in the land. People would gather to watch her as she sat at her spinning-wheel and spun the soft, many-colored wools into fine, even threads, and then wove them on her loom into a web enchanting both to the sight and to the touch. Most marvelous of all it was to see her take her needle and cover the web with pictures such as glow on the canvas of a great painter. Her lovely, smiling face, her white arms and slender, graceful body were as pleasant to look upon as the pictures she created. Nymphs[3] stole[4] from the streams and the woods, and stood on tiptoe looking over the shoulders of the mortals, marveling at Arachne's wonderful skill.

"Athene herself must have taught her!" exclaimed an admiring onlooker one day.

Arachne turned round quickly. Her face was not so beautiful now, there was such an ugly look of pride and scorn[5] upon it.

"Athene teach me, indeed! My skill is equal to hers, and that I would prove if she would match herself against me."

The hearers cried out in astonishment and alarm that a mortal should speak in such terms of the great goddess.

---

3. **nymphs** (nimfs): young and beautiful nature goddesses.

4. **stole:** crept secretly.

5. **scorn** (skôrn): feeling of anger or disgust.

But Arachne held to what she had said, and repeated it again and again to other listeners, until all through the land it was known that the boastful maiden had challenged Athene to a contest. Soon the goddess herself heard of it, and though she was very much displeased, she resolved to warn the girl and give her a chance to escape the punishment she deserved.

> **"Maiden," said the old woman kindly, ". . . Boast if you will that no mortal can excel you, but do not match yourself against the high gods."**

So, taking the form of an old woman, Athene joined the group assembled to watch Arachne at work. Quietly she made her way to the girl's side.

"Is it true that you have said that your skill is equal to Athene's?" she asked.

"Indeed it is," answered the girl proudly, "and I only wish she could hear me. If she should beat me in the trial I should be quite willing to pay the penalty."

"Maiden," said the old woman kindly, "listen to the words of one who has lived long in the world and seen much. Boast if you will that no mortal can excel you, but do not match yourself against the high gods. Rather, ask pardon of Athene for your presumptuous[6] words. She will forgive you if your repentance is sincere."

Arachne was very angry, and spoke rudely to the old woman. "Keep your advice for those who ask it," she said; "as for me, I repeat that my greatest wish is that Athene should come and let me show what I can do."

"Athene is here," said the old woman, in tones that startled the graceless girl. She turned and saw a tall and

---

6. **presumptuous** (prē·zump'chōō·əs): overly confident; arrogant.

gracious figure with noble brow, and deep gray eyes that looked sternly upon her. For a moment she was overawed, but quickly recovered herself and spoke boldly.

"Then I say once more that I am ready for the contest."

The looms were set up and the goddess and the maiden began their work. The bystanders bent in awe before Athene, then watched silently as the deft[7] fingers of the two weavers moved swiftly among wools of rare and brilliant dyes. Soon the pictures began to grow before them. Arachne's showed a sunlit stretch of sea where swelling waves tumbled and splashed so that the onlookers almost felt the salt spray in their faces. Swimming among the waves was a magnificent white bull, his golden horns, round which were twined a careless garland of meadow flowers, glinting in the sun. On his back, holding to one of his horns, lay a girl. Her eyes were wide with fear, but it seemed that the cry of terror coming from her parted lips was arrested as she

---

7. **deft** (deft): sure; skillful.

Striking Garb

Pallas Athene (known as Minerva to the Romans) was the Greek goddess of war, wisdom, and crafts. She is said to have been born when the great god Zeus split open his forehead, and out she came—full-grown and dressed for battle. Athene's armor is usually shown to include a helmet, a spear and shield, and her father's famous breastplate, the *aegis* (ē'jis). This leather breastplate is covered in goatskins and fringed with snakes. In its center rests the likeness of Medusa, which was said to turn onlookers into stone. When shaken, the breastplate supposedly cast thunderbolts from all sides—a fearsome garment, indeed.

bent her head to listen to the words of the lordly bull, while a faint flush was creeping back into her whitened cheeks. The girl was Europa and the bull was Zeus himself, who had taken that form because he wished to woo the maiden unnoted by Hera's jealous eye.

Arachne knew, even before she heard the delighted and astonished cries of those who watched, that this was the best piece of work she had ever done. She turned triumphantly and looked at the web of Athene. Then her heart sank, for, conceited as she was, she was yet a true artist, and she recognized that here was work beyond anything that she could accomplish.

Athene had chosen as the subject of her picture the contest that she had held, in the presence of Zeus and all the dwellers on Olympus, with Poseidon, god of the sea. Zeus had decreed that a new and beautiful city, lately founded in Greece, should bear the name of whichever deity could produce the gift most useful to man, and Athene and Poseidon met in rivalry for the honor which both coveted.[8]

Poseidon struck the ground with his trident, and a horse, finely formed, noble and spirited, sprang up. The assembled gods shouted in delight, and declared that nothing Athene could produce could surpass this wonderful animal. When Athene, in her turn, caused an olive-tree

▲ Arachne weaving cloth on her loom.

---

8. **coveted** (kuv'it•id): desired greatly.

to spring up, there were cries of derision and scornful laughter. The goddess, unmoved, proceeded to explain the manifold[9] uses of the tree; and when she had finished, the assembled gods agreed that it was far more valuable than the horse of Poseidon. The city was therefore called Athens.

All this Athene had shown upon her web, with the details as lovely and as lifelike as in the picture of Arachne; but here was a radiance and a glory which clearly showed that the work was done by no mortal hand. The onlookers had admired the web of Arachne; they were awed and enraptured by that of Athene.

No need to ask who was the victor. Arachne knew only too well. She felt she could not live to bear the humiliation she had brought upon herself. A rope was hanging from a beam above her head; she seized it and drew a noose about her neck, intending to hang herself.

But Athene would not allow her thus to perish. "Live," commanded the goddess, "that you may be a warning for all time to those who bear themselves proudly toward the high gods. Live, and spin and weave without ceasing; not as you will, but in the way that the gods have chosen."

She raised her hand and sprinkled upon the girl a few drops of the juice of aconite.[10] At once the lovely colors died out of the maiden's face and hair and hands, and they became a dingy gray. Her head, limbs, and body shrank until only a tiny gray mass was left; her fingers grew thread-like and stood out round this gray mass raising and supporting it. Arachne had become a spider.

---

9. **manifold** (man'ə•fōld'): many.

10. **aconite** (ak'ə•nĭt'): poisonous plant called monkshood.

Curse of the Spider Woman

Thanks to Arachne, spiders are known in the scientific world as *arachnids.* Their more common name comes from the Old English word *spinnan,* meaning "to spin." Although most people dislike—or even fear—these eight-legged critters, few spiders are harmful to humans. They prefer to attack insects, trapping them in their webs and then feasting on them in a gruesome process. First, a spider grips its prey and injects a digestive fluid into its body. This fluid breaks down the insect's body tissues and turns them to liquid. The spider then sucks the liquid into its own abdomen, which can store the meal for many days. Other habits of the spider are far less frightful. Its ability to spin a web, for example, is a curious and amazing feat. The web begins in the spider's body as a liquid but is passed out as a solid. It can be very fine, or, in some cases, as strong as steel piano wire! As wily hunters and expert weavers, these creatures—along with Arachne herself—are perhaps not as cursed as one might think.

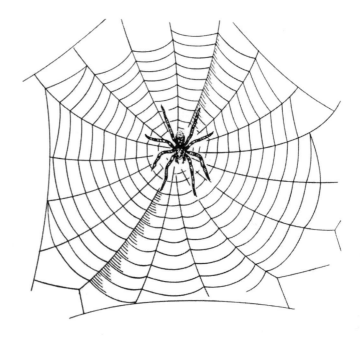

Who's Who?

Now that you have come to the end of the Greco-Roman myths in this collection, here is a chart that will help you remember the gods and goddesses you have met.

Greek Name	Roman Name	Description
Zeus (zōōs)	Jupiter (Jove) (jōō'pit•ər, jōv)	king of the gods; ruler of the sky and the weather
Cronus (krō'nəs)	Saturn (sat'ərn)	ruler of the Titans
Hera (hir'ə)	Juno (jōō'nō)	queen of the gods; protector of women and marriage
Poseidon (pō•sī'dən)	Neptune (nep'tōōn')	god of the sea
Demeter (di•mēt'ər)	Ceres (sir'ēz')	goddess of grain and fruit
Persephone (pər•sef'ə•nē)	Proserpina (prō•sʉr'pi•nə)	goddess of spring and the underworld; daughter of Demeter
Hades, Pluto (hā'dēz', plōōt'ō)	Pluto (plōōt'ō)	god of the underworld
Eros (er'äs')	Cupid (kyōō'pid)	god of love; son of Aphrodite
Aphrodite (af'rə•dīt'ē)	Venus (vē'nəs)	goddess of love and beauty
Athene, Athena, Pallas Athene (pal'əs ə•thē'nə)	Minerva (mi•nʉr'və)	goddess of wisdom, arts, crafts, and war; protector of the city of Athens

When we say that someone has "become a different person," we usually mean that his or her personality has changed. Witnessing such a change can be painful. However, what if a loved one *really* turned into a different person? The following Japanese folk tale gives us a literal look at this familiar cliché.

The Snow Woman

RAFE MARTIN

Long ago, a poor woodcutter and his mother lived in a little hut at the forest's edge.

Every day he went into the forest and chopped down dead trees. He'd lop off the dead branches, cut the wood to even lengths, and tie it into bundles. Then he would carry it back to the village to sell for firewood. In this way he supported his mother and himself.

One winter a bad storm buried the village in snow. The wood that could be cut near the village had already been taken. So when there was a lull in the storm, the young woodcutter set out into the forest with an old woodcutter from the village. They cut down a good-sized tree and trimmed the branches. As they worked, snow began to fall. Quickly they tied up the cut wood, hefted it onto their backs, and, bent under their loads, headed for home.

You Need to Know...

Folk tales were originally "tell-aloud" stories created by ordinary people and passed down from generation to generation. They usually follow a set pattern, or formula, which makes them easy to remember.

Some elements of the folk tale may vary from culture to culture. In Japan, the formula looks like this:

- The story begins and ends with set phrases, much like "Once upon a time" and "They lived happily ever after."
- The plot is simple and straightforward.
- Only two characters usually appear in any given scene. These characters usually have opposite natures, such as mortal and immortal or young and old.
- Folk tales must be told after dark.

During the mid-1900s, a Japanese folk tale buff began collecting the folk tales of Japan. During his research, he encountered at least a dozen storytellers who claimed to know over one hundred tales! Little wonder that folk tale formulas came in handy for wordsmiths such as these.

The wind blew and the snow whirled around them. Great white flakes blew against their eyes like feathers so that they could hardly see, and the wind cut through their straw capes right to the bone. As they staggered on, the drifts piled up around them. In no time the trails were completely buried. The two men were lost and night was falling. They needed to find shelter soon or they would die. They came to a river with ice floating in the water. They would freeze if they tried to swim across. Then just ahead along the shore, they saw an old, abandoned fisherman's hut. They stumbled in, exhausted, and propped the door closed behind them with a piece of wood. But the hut was so old the wind just blew through the cracks in the walls. They stacked the wood they had cut in a pile around their bodies to keep that cold wind from them. At last, shivering and shaking in the darkness, they drifted off to sleep.

Around midnight the young woodcutter awoke. The door of the hut was open. The wind had stopped blowing. All was quiet and still. And standing there in the moonlight was a beautiful woman. Her face, her hands, and her robe were white as the snow, while her eyes and hair were black as night. The young woodcutter thought he must be dreaming.

Then the woman glided silently forward. It was as if her feet were not moving at all, or as if she had no feet. She approached the old woodcutter, knelt beside him, and breathed upon him. Her breath was like smoke, and as she breathed, the young woodcutter heard a sound like the whistling of the snow-laden wind. *Whoooooowhhhhh.* And wherever that breath touched, ice began to form. When she was done, the old man was frozen and dead.

Now the woman rose and glided toward the young woodcutter. She knelt beside him, bringing her pale, beautiful face closer and closer. The young man turned away. A tear trickled from his eye and ran down along his cheek. Then the pale woman smiled, and when she smiled the woodcutter could see her teeth. They were long and clear and pointed as icicles. In a voice soft as the falling snow, she said, "You are so young, so young. And so handsome. I shall spare you. BUT," she added, and the icy tone of her voice now made his blood freeze, "tell no one, not even your mother, of what you have seen this night. If you ever tell I shall instantly know of it. Then I shall return and make you wish that you had died this night with the old man there." Outside, the wind howled and the door pounded back and forth. She

Boo Who?

In this "chilling" scene, the Snow Woman seems nothing short of a ghost. She arrives, as ghosts often do, at midnight, and she comes dressed in the traditional white robe. She even emits a ghostly moan! Ghost stories exist in virtually all cultures and in many forms—short stories, poems, novels, and campfire tales, to name just a few. Ghost stories probably thrive because they give human beings a glimpse of the mysterious "beyond." They are also a handy way to keep friends and loved ones from passing *too* far away. Abraham Lincoln, for example, is said by many to haunt the White House. He's been known to knock on doors, stare out windows, recline on beds—that kind of thing. Many of these stories seem almost believable, especially when you learn that Lincoln himself had a vision of his own funeral shortly before his death. However, it is also true that when this beloved president was shot, most U.S. citizens were not ready to say goodbye. Seeing his "ghost" might be their way—and ours—of keeping our hero here.

rose, glided silently over the floor, through the opened door, and was gone. The young woodcutter rushed to the door. He wedged it tightly closed again. Then he lay in the corner, shaking and shaking.

The villagers found him in the morning white with fear and the old man dead. They brought the young woodcutter back to the village, but he would not speak about the events of that night. And all that winter he refused to go back into those woods. But when spring came and the blossoms were forming, the leaves opening, the green grass growing, and the birds singing, the young wood-cutter regained his courage. Once more he lifted up his ax and set out into the forest to cut down the dead trees, lop off the dead branches, and bring the wood home to support his mother and himself.

One spring evening as the young woodcutter was returning to his village with a bundle of wood on his back, he met a young woman. She was pale, slender, and pretty. She told him that her parents had died and that now she was journeying to a distant city to find work with relatives there.

The young woodcutter said to her, "A young, attractive girl like you should not travel alone through this forest at night. There are robbers, bandits, rough, cruel men in these woods and . . . and worse. No. You must come back with me to the hut where I live with my old mother. You shall eat with us and spend the night in safety. Then in the morning, if you must go, you may walk through these woods when the sun is bright."

So she went with him. She said her name was Yuke, which means snow, and that she was grateful for his kindness. The woodcutter's old mother liked Yuke, and Yuke seemed completely at home in the little hut with the woodcutter and his mother. When the sun rose that morning, it was clear that she would not be leaving for she and the young woodcutter were already in love. Soon they married. In time they raised a family, two boys and a girl. When at last the old mother died, she died happily, for her life had been good. She had

Sealed Fate

If you want to be a shape-shifter, say the experts, there are three ways to do it. One is to be a sorcerer and learn the correct spell. Another is to be put under a spell. The third is to be born with the ability to change shape, by chance or by will. This last alternative may sound fun, but what if you got stuck in a shape you did not permanently want? Such perils are the stuff of folk tales. Some werewolf stories, for example, feature young men who sprout claws and whiskers at every full moon, like it or not. Other milder tales, such as "The Snow Woman," are wistful stories in which a female shape-shifter takes on human form for the sake of love. In one such Icelandic tale, a seal-woman sheds her skin and swims as a maiden among the rocks. When a man steals her skin, the maiden is forced to marry him in order to survive. By accident, the woman rediscovers her skin years later and, with bittersweet joy, reclaims her true form.

had a fine daughter-in-law and beautiful grandchildren. And the woodcutter? Why, he was happy too. His wife was indeed beautiful. And not just her face but even her heart and spirit seemed beautiful. And then too she seemed to stay as young-looking and as beautiful as the day he had first met her. Or so it seemed to him.

One winter's night near the New Year, the woodcutter and his wife sat together making gifts for the children. Though they had little money, their love was strong and they were capable people. What money could not provide they would make themselves. The woodcutter was weaving straw sandals for the children while his wife sewed little kimonos.

As Yuke sewed, the pale light from the oil lamp fell on her face. Glancing at her for a moment, the woodcutter appeared startled. She smiled at him. "What is it, dear husband?"

"Oh," he said strangely, "I had forgotten."

"Forgotten what?" she asked.

"Once," he answered slowly, "years ago, maybe it was a dream, I cannot be sure now for it was so long ago—once I think I saw a woman as pale and as beautiful as you look in the lamplight now."

"Oh," his wife said, pausing in her sewing, "tell me about it."

▲ Japanese kimonos.

And the woodcutter began to tell her of that night long ago when the woman of the snows had entered the hut, breathed upon the old man, and frozen him dead.

As he told the tale his wife sat up straighter. Though she continued her sewing, with his every word her face became more solemn and grave.

When he was done with the story, she had finished the last of the little robes. She bit the thread. Tenderly she placed the little kimono down upon the tatami[1] matting beside the others she had already finished. She smoothed the little kimonos with a pale, graceful hand. Outside the wind began to blow. She rose to her feet. Her face turned white as the snows. Her hands turned white as the snows. Her robe too became all white.

She glided across the floor toward the wood-cutter, who sat as if frozen, his eyes wide with disbelief and fear. "No dream!" she wailed. "It was I that night long ago. And I told you to tell no one! And now that you have told I should kill you most horribly, just as I promised. But no, I can-not. Ah, the pity of it!

---

1. **tatami** (tə•tä′mē): rice straw.

The spell is broken. I can no longer remain. Why did you speak? Because of this I must leave you, must leave my home and children." Turning toward the room where the children slept, she whispered as the wind continued to rise outside, "Be well, my dear little ones. I shall always watch over you." Then looking at the woodcutter, she hissed in a voice like blowing snow, "But I warn you. Care for our children well! For if I ever learn that you have harmed so much as a single hair of their heads, I shall return and do as I promised."

She glided soundlessly toward the door. Outside the wind howled. The door blew open and she glided through, rose up into the howling wind and storm, and was gone.

Now all that was long, long ago. Still, if you listen some winter's night as the wind comes moaning through the trees, you may hear a voice on the wind. It's the voice of the snow woman, yearning for her lost children and home.

The Weeping Woman of the Night

Weeping women do not haunt Japanese folklore alone. In Mexico and the American Southwest, a figure known as *La Llorona* (Spanish for "weeping woman") is known for her similar plight. The story goes like this: A woman is betrayed by her husband. She turns her anger upon her children and, in a fit of insanity, drowns them in a lake or river. The ruined mother soon dies of a broken heart—but does not fade away altogether. Clothed in a gown of white, her ghost is said to appear along the darkened banks of rivers, crying in eerie strains of grief. Versions of this story exist in Europe, too. There, legendary "women in white" are said to have once roamed freely at night, when they should have been at home. In spite of the differences between the Japanese, Mexican American, and European tales, all three have one thing in common: The women continue to grieve in the darkness of the night.

Everyone has special skills and talents. However, when we regard one of our skills too highly—or use it in a way that we should not—somebody usually steps in to put us back in our place. The following African folk tale gives this ancient truth a beastly new twist.

A Man Who Could Transform Himself

JOHN S. MBITI

There was a man called Mbokothe, and he had a brother. The two were orphans and they lived together. Their parents had left them two cows when they died, and one day, Mbokothe said to his brother, "Let me take these two cows and go to a medicine man, so that he can give me some treatment, the giving of magical powers." And his elder brother told him to take them.

Mbokothe led the two cows out of their home, and drove them to a famous medicine man in another part of the country. The medicine man treated him, and gave him magical powers, so that he could transform himself into any kind of animal that he wanted. He returned to his home, told his brother about it, and said, "If I change into an animal, don't tell anyone my secret."

One day Mbokothe transformed himself into a huge bull, and his brother drove him to the market to sell him. All the

You Need to Know...

In many societies, the medicine man or woman—also called the shaman—is not only a doctor, but also a kind of priest, wizard, and wonderworker. With close ties to the world of spirits, these shamans have special knowledge that other people do not possess. They can use plants, herbs, and sacred objects to heal wounds or illnesses. They can also lead elaborate rituals to treat the sick or to communicate with the spirits. Some medicine men and women receive their powers directly from the gods. Others are schooled in the arts of healing and then are able to pass these skills on to worthy pupils. Abusing the powers of the shaman is frowned upon by both people and gods—as this story goes to show.

people that saw them stopped and stared, wondering where such a big bull had come from. One man came looking to buy and he asked how much that big bull cost. The brother told him that he would exchange it for two cows and five goats. So the man bought the bull, intending to slaughter it to impress the man whose daughter he wanted to marry.

The buyer drove the bull towards his home, but before they got there, the bull escaped and ran away. The man chased after it, with no luck, until he was exhausted. The bull transformed itself so that one half of it looked like a lion, and then disappeared into the forest. The man followed its trail and saw on the ground the prints of a lion's paw, and he exclaimed, "It has already been eaten by a lion!" So he went back home, upset at having wasted so much time and energy. The bull went on, and when it was far from where people lived, it transformed itself back into a man, and Mbokothe returned home and saw the cows and goats that his brother had obtained from the market that day.

On another market day, these two brothers did the same thing, and again Mbokothe transformed himself into a bull. His brother sold him for ten goats, and drove the goats back to their home while Mbokothe was being driven to the home of the man who bought him. But to their misfortune, the man who bought the bull had also been to the medicine man, and had himself gotten a powerful charm. When they came near the house of the man, the bull ran off, as on the previous occasion, and the owner chased it towards the forest. He came very near to catching it, and Mbokothe decided to transform himself into a lion, thinking that the man would be scared if he saw a lion, but the other man was also able to change into a lion, and continued to chase Mbokothe. When Mbokothe saw that he was about to be caught, he transformed himself into a bird and flew away. But the other man changed into a kite,[1] and then both of them flew in the sky, chasing each other.

Again, Mbokothe saw that he was on the point of being caught, so he came down to the ground, changed himself into an antelope, and continued to run. His pursuer changed into a wolf, and the two ran on till at last Mbokothe yielded, and said to the other man, after they had both changed back into human beings, "Okay, let's go to my home and I'll give you back your goats." They went to his home and Mbokothe gave the man his ten goats. For he knew that he had met his match in making magic.

Now You See Them . . .

The first shape-shifting gods and spirits are thought to have created the world. Here is a look at a few of these morphing masters.

- **Dxui** was the shape-shifting creator in myths of the African Bush people. He made everything that exists by becoming one thing after the other. Every tree, insect, and pebble was thought to be the fingerprint of Dxui himself.
- **Proteus,** a Greek god of the sea, could shape-shift *and* tell the future. People often sought his wisdom, but Proteus would change shapes in order to avoid their questions. To catch him, a mortal had to grasp the napping god and hold him tightly—whether he became a lion, serpent, or boar—until Proteus wearied of the game.
- The African shape-changer **Anansi** was also a mischievous trickster. He had the ability to take on any form he chose, although his favorite was that of a human or spider. Anansi was brought to the Americas by enslaved Africans, and here became known as **Annency.**

---

1. kite (kīt): a kind of bird.

Why would a princess *ever* kiss a frog? According to this Chinese folk tale, she would not—unless, of course, he looked like a prince to begin with.

The Frog Who Became an Emperor

Once upon a time there lived a very poor couple. A baby was on the way when the husband was forced to leave his home to find a living somewhere far away. Before he left, he embraced his wife fondly and looked long at her. Then he gave her the last few silver pieces he had, saying, "When the child is born, be it a boy or a girl, you must do all you can to bring it up. You and I are so poor that there is no hope for us now. But our child may be able to help us make a living."

Three months after her husband's departure, the wife gave birth. The baby was neither a boy nor a little girl, but a frog!

The poor mother was heartbroken, and wept bitterly.

"Ah, a water creature, not a child!" she cried. "Our hopes for someone to care for us in our old age are gone! How can I ever face people again!"

She thought at first she would do away with the frog, but she did not have the heart to do so.

You Need to Know...

In a sense, frogs and other amphibians are the shape-shifters of nature. It is no surprise, then, that they often show up as the shape-shifters of folklore as well. These scaleless animals live part of their lives in water and part on land. Most amphibians (with the exception of the frog in this story!) hatch from eggs laid in water or moist ground. They remain there for a time as *larvae,* meaning "young." Gradually, through the process of *metamorphosis,* the larvae transform into very different-looking adults. As grown-ups, amphibians keep some of their shape-shifting qualities. Although they do not literally change shape, some can change color with variations in light or temperature. Because they are coldblooded, their body temperature can also change to match that of their surroundings. One part of the adaptable amphibian is rigid, however. Much like the strong-willed hero of this Chinese tale, all amphibians come equipped with a backbone.

She wanted to bring it up, but was afraid of what the neighbors would say.

As she brooded[1] over the matter, she remembered her husband's words before he went away, and she decided not to kill the frog but to keep it hidden under the bed. In this way, no one knew she had given birth to a frog-child. But within two months, the frog had grown so big that he could no longer be kept under the bed. One day, he suddenly spoke in a human voice.

"Mother," he said, "my father is coming back tonight. I am going to wait for him beside the road."

And sure enough, the husband did come home that very night.

"Have you seen your son?" the wife asked anxiously.

"Where? Where is my son?"

"He was waiting for you by the side of the road. Didn't you see him?"

"No! I saw no sign of anyone," her husband answered, surprised. "All I saw was an awful frog which gave me a fright."

"That frog was your son," said the wife unhappily.

When the husband heard that his wife had given birth to a frog, he was grieved.

"Why did you tell him to meet me?" he said. "Wasn't that a strange thing to do?"

"What do you mean, tell him to meet you? He went without any telling from me. He suddenly said you were coming tonight and went out to meet you."

"This is really extraordinary," thought the husband, brightening up. "No one knew I was coming. How could he have known?"

"Call him home, quickly," he said aloud. "He might catch cold outside."

---

1. **brooded** (br$\overline{oo}$d'id): worried about.

Just as the mother opened the door to do so, the frog came in. He hopped over to his father, who asked him, "Was it you I met on the road?"

"Yes," said the frog. "I was waiting for you, Father."

"How did you know I was coming back tonight?"

"I know everything under heaven."

The father and mother were amazed by his words and more amazed when he went on.

"Our country is in great peril," he said solemnly. "We are unable to resist the invaders. I want Father to take me to the emperor, for I must save our country."

"How can that be?" said the father. "Firstly, you have no horse. Secondly, you have no weapons, and thirdly, you have never been on a battlefield. How, then, do you propose to fight?"

The frog was very much in earnest. "Only take me there," he pleaded. "I'll defeat the enemy, never fear."

The father could not dissuade the frog, so he took his frog-son to the city to seek an audience with the emperor. After two days' journey, they arrived at the capital, where they saw the Imperial Decree displayed.

"The imperial capital is in danger. My country has been invaded. We are willing to marry our daughter to the man who can drive away the enemy. . . ."

Froggy Folk Tales

Like so many other tales, this froggy folk tale seems to have leapt in one form or another across the globe. The version you probably know (which comes from Europe) begins when a princess tosses her golden ball down a well. A frog appears and promises to retrieve it if the girl will marry him. The princess agrees, but when the frog succeeds, she grabs the ball and flees. The scorned frog shows up at her palace that night, reminding the girl of her promise. In some stories, the princess lets the frog sleep on her pillow. In others, she throws him against the wall. However, in both cases, the frog is transformed into a handsome prince. Unlike the Chinese princess in this selection, the princess in the more familiar version matures during the course of the story. At the beginning she is a little girl with a toy, and at the end she is a woman with strength and courage. For this transformation she is richly rewarded. Still, both versions of the tale do share a common moral: Be prepared to keep the promises you make!

The frog stretched out his hand, tore down the decree and with one gulp swallowed it. The soldier guarding the Imperial Decree was greatly alarmed. He could hardly imagine a frog accepting such a responsible duty. However, since the frog had swallowed the decree, he must be taken into the palace.

The emperor asked the frog if he had the means and ability to defeat the enemy. The frog replied, "Yes, Lord." Then the emperor asked him how many men and horses he would need.

"Not a single horse or a single man," answered the frog. "All I need is a heap of hot, glowing embers."

The emperor immediately commanded that a heap of hot, glowing embers be brought and it was done. Flickering flames from the embers leaped high into the air and the heat was intense. The frog sat before the fire devouring the flames by the mouthful for three days and three nights. He ate till his belly was as big and round as a bladder[2] full of fat. By now the city was in great danger, for the enemy was already at the walls. The emperor was terribly apprehensive, but the frog behaved as if nothing unusual was happening, and calmly went on swallowing fire and flame. Only after the third day had passed did he go to the top of the city wall and look at the situation. There, ringing the city, were thousands of soldiers and horses in serried[3] ranks, as far as the eye could see.

"Now, frog, how are you going to drive back the enemy?" asked the emperor.

"Order your troops to stop using their bows," replied the frog. "And open the city gate."

---

2. **bladder** (blad'ər): bag made from animal membrane.
3. **serried** (ser'ēd): close together.

The emperor turned pale with alarm when he heard these words.

"What! With the enemy at our very door! You tell me to open the gate! How dare you trifle with me?"

"Your Imperial Highness has bidden me drive the enemy away," said the frog. "And that being so, you must heed[4] my words."

The emperor was helpless. He ordered the soldiers to stop bending their bows, lay down their arrows and throw open the gate.

As soon as the gate was flung open, the invaders poured in. The frog was above them in the gate-tower and, as they passed underneath, he coolly and calmly spat fire down on them, searing[5] countless men and horses. They fled back in disorder.

---

4. **heed** (hēd): be aware of; notice.
5. **searing** (sir'iŋ): burning at a high temperature.

Uphill Battle

Even without a fire-eating frog, the emperor's enemies would have had difficulty attacking the walled city. One way to attack an ancient fortress was to climb over the walls with ladders. However, the climber could not defend himself from the rocks, arrows, or hot tar thrown down on him. Another form of attack was the battering ram, a heavy wooden beam that was pounded into walls and gates by running men. This weapon did not work well on hilltop structures or on castles with moats. Other, more complex weapons included the catapult (like a giant bow and arrow) and the belfroy, a rolling mini-fortress complete with its own drawbridge. Many of these weapons took a long time to build and operate and were difficult to use in surprise attacks. Overall, ancient warfare was a cumbersome, difficult business. Imagine the delight of the emperor's enemies when the gates were opened wide for them!

The emperor was overjoyed when he saw that the enemy was defeated. He made the frog a general and ordered that the victory should be celebrated for several days. But of the princess he said nothing. To tell the truth, he had not the slightest intention of letting his daughter marry a frog.

"Of course I cannot do such a thing!" he said to himself. Instead, he let it be known that it was the princess who refused. She must marry someone else, but whom? He did not know what to do. Anyone but a frog! Finally he ordained that her marriage should be decided by casting the Embroidered Ball.

Casting the Embroidered Ball! The news spread immediately throughout the whole country and within a few days the city was in a turmoil. Men from far and wide came to try their luck, and all manner of people flocked to the capital. The day came. The frog was present. He did not push his way into the mob but stood at the very edge of the crowded square.

A gaily festooned pavilion of a great height had been built. The emperor led the princess and her train of maids, dressed in scarlet and green, to their seats high up on the stand.

The moment arrived. The princess tossed the Embroidered Ball into the air, and down it gently floated. The masses in the square surged and roared like a raging sea. As one and all stretched eager hands to clutch the ball, the frog drew in a mighty breath and, like a whirling tornado, sucked the ball straight to him.

Now, surely, the princess will have to marry the frog! But the emperor was still unwilling to let this happen.

"An Embroidered Ball cast by a princess," he declared, "can only be seized by a human hand. No other creature may take it."

He told the princess to throw down a second ball.

This time a young, stalwart fellow caught the ball.

"This is the man!" cried the happy emperor. "Here is the person fit to be my imperial son-in-law."

A sumptuous feast was set to celebrate the occasion.

Can you guess who that young, stalwart fellow was? Of course it was the frog, now in the guise**6** of a man.

---

6. **guise** (gīz): outer appearance.

Grand Illusions

Like the frog in this tale, ancient Chinese emperors had grand expectations—and used all of their powers to realize them. Qin Shi Huang, the first Chinese emperor, is a good example. During his short reign (221–207 B.C.), this young ruler unified China into a single nation. He built the Great Wall of China. He wrote laws, laid out roads, and created a money system—all pretty remarkable feats for a young man. However, perhaps his most striking achievement was the tomb he created for himself. This tomb, discovered in 1974, took about four decades and 700,000 slaves to build. The main tomb (not yet excavated) is said to contain a ceiling adorned with starry pearls, a stone floor inlaid with rivers and miniature oceans, and a collection of tiny palaces and parks. In vaults near the main tomb, more than 6,000 life-size pottery soldiers, servants, and horses were discovered. Poised for battle, these ghostly figures were created to escort the ambitious emperor into the realm of the dead.

Not till he was married to the princess did he change back again. By day he was a frog but at night he stripped off his green skin and was transformed into a fine, upstanding youth.

The princess could not keep it a secret and one day revealed it to her father, the emperor. He was startled but happy.

"At night," he said to his son-in-law, "you discard your outer garment, I hear, and become a handsome young man. Why do you wear that horrid frog-skin in the day?"

"Ah, Sire," replied the frog, "this outer garment is priceless. When I wear it in winter, I am warm and cozy; and in summer, cool and fresh. It is proof against wind and rain. Not even the fiercest flame can set it alight. And as long as I wear it, I can live for thousands of years."

"Let me try it on!" demanded the emperor.

"Yes, Sire," replied the frog and made haste to discard his skin.

The emperor smiled gleefully. He took off his dragon-embroidered robe and put on the frog-skin. But then he could not take it off again!

The frog put on the imperial robe and became the emperor. His father-in-law remained a frog forever.

Read On

The Peacock Maiden: Folk Tales from China, compiled by Nicholas Van Rijn (University Press of the Pacific), *The Man Who Tricked a Ghost* by Laurence Yep (Troll), and *Cow-Tail Switch and other West African Stories* by Harold Courlander and George Herzog (Henry Holt) will give you more stories from China and Africa. For additional tales of mystery and transformation from Japan, read *Mysterious Tales of Japan* by Rafe Martin (Putnam) and *The Magic Listening Cap* by Yoshiko Uchida (Creative Arts).

CHAPTER 5

Foolishness and Trickery

Make It or Break It

We like to believe that life is reasonable and that we are in control. However, the fool and the trickster remind us that this isn't always so. These mischievous "chaos creators" teach us through humor, because comic situations can express truths we might otherwise find hard to swallow.

• In many stories the rabbit or hare appears as the trickster. From the tales of Brer Rabbit to the film escapades of Bugs Bunny, the rabbit trickster has won the hearts of his audience. His popular message? Every battle can be won—and be enjoyable, too.

• Coyote is a master trickster of American Indian tales. His Hollywood cousin, Wile E. Coyote, shows us another aspect of the coyote trickster. Repeatedly flattened, crinkled, and tricked by his own devices, he is always back in a flash—as good as new and none the wiser.

The Granger Collection, New York

▲ Brer Rabbit.

Not Out of the Woods Yet

Fairy tales are as indestructible and enduring as the hardy young fool characters who are often their heroes. Consider the ways we keep fairy tales alive today:

• Each year, millions of people wander the halls of fairy tale castles, sharing the adventures of Pinocchio and Peter Pan and getting their photos taken with

Memorable Quote

"He who asks a question is a fool for five minutes; he who does not ask a question remains a fool forever."

—Chinese Proverb

▲ Rapunzel.

INVESTIGATE:

What other tricky and foolish characters have you found in your reading or film and TV viewing?

storybook characters. Where? At the numerous theme parks across the country.

• Fairy tales have been the inspiration for numerous plays, musicals, movies, and operas. The opera *Hansel and Gretel* is regularly performed for both children and adults. "Cinderella" has been filmed numerous times since silent film days. *Into the Woods,* a fairy tale musical, has a cast that includes Rapunzel, Jack (of beanstalk fame), Little Red Riding Hood, and other legendary figures who wander the woods, singing catchy tunes and getting tangled up in each other's tales.

Too Bad to Be True?

The selections in this chapter include fables and other brief stories that teach a lesson. Some of the oldest "teaching tales" are cautionary tales—stories that caution, or warn, against certain behaviors. Today, a new kind of cautionary tale, the "urban legend," is constantly being created and passed around by mouth, in print, and even over the Internet. These "urban legends" are funny, morbid, or shocking stories that are *almost* too far-fetched to be true. Stories about alligators in the sewers, mice in soda bottles, a dangerous person hiding in the back seat of a car, and bogus e-mail viruses, for example, encourage us all to be more careful. But they also send some serious shivers down our spines.

If you've ever played a trick on someone, you know that there's usually a price to be paid. For example, you may suffer from your own guilt—or from the other person's anger. In the following Norse myth, we see that even trickster gods must sometimes make amends for their mischief.

Sif's Golden Hair

PADRAIC COLUM

All who dwelt in Asgard,[1] the Aesir[2] and the Asyniur, who were the Gods and the Goddesses, and the Vanir,[3] who were the friends of the Gods and the Goddesses, were wroth[4] with Loki.[5] It was no wonder they were wroth with him, for he had let the Giant Thiassi carry off Idun[6] and her golden apples. Still, it must be told that the show they made of their wrath made Loki ready to do more mischief in Asgard.

One day he saw a chance to do mischief that made his heart rejoice. Sif, the wife of Thor, was laying asleep outside her house. Her beautiful golden hair flowed all round her. Loki knew how much Thor loved that shining hair, and how greatly Sif prized it because of Thor's love.

---

1. **Asgard** (äs'gärd') in Norse mythology, the home of gods and slain heroes.

2. **Aesir** (ā'sir).

3. **Vanir** (vä'nir).

4. **wroth** (rôth): angry.

5. **Loki** (lō'kē): Norse god who creates mischief.

6. **Idun** (ē'dōōn): Norse goddess of spring.

You Need to Know...

Like other tricksters, Loki is a bundle of contradictions. At once clever and foolish, Loki's outlandish ideas typically backfire. Take the building of the Asgard wall, for example. When the Norse gods desired a wall to protect their realm, a horseman offered to build it in exchange for Freya, the goddess of beauty. Loki urged the gods to accept the terms, but only if the wall were completed in six months—an impossible task. With the help of his horse, the man nearly succeeded, and the gods grew increasingly worried. To fix his mistake, Loki disguised himself as a mare and lured the horse away. Enraged, the builder revealed himself to be not a man, but a giant—a dangerous enemy of the gods. Too close for comfort? For the other gods, yes; but for Loki, no. As you will see, this fire-god trickster loves nothing so much as—well, as playing with fire.

▲ Thor.

Here was his chance to do a great mischief. Smilingly, he took out his shears and he cut off the shining hair, every strand and every tress. She did not waken while her treasure was being taken from her. But Loki left Sif's head cropped and bare.

Thor was away from Asgard. Coming back to the City of the Gods, he went into his house. Sif, his wife, was not there to welcome him. He called to Sif, but no glad answer came from her. To the palaces of all the Gods and Goddesses Thor went, but in none of them did he find Sif, his golden-haired wife.

When he was coming back to his house he heard his name whispered. He stopped, and then a figure stole out from behind a stone. A veil covered her head, and Thor scarce knew that this was Sif, his wife. As he went to her she sobbed and sobbed. "O Thor, my husband," she said, "do not look upon me. I am ashamed that you should see me. I shall go from Asgard and from the company of the Gods and Goddesses, and I shall go down to Svartheim and live amongst the Dwarfs. I cannot bear that any of the Dwellers in Asgard should look upon me now."

"O Sif," cried Thor, "what has happened to change you?"

"I have lost the hair of my head," said Sif, "I have lost the beautiful golden hair that you, Thor, loved. You will not love me any more, and so I must go away, down to Svartheim and to the company of the Dwarfs. They are as ugly as I am now."

Then she took the veil off her head and Thor saw that all her beautiful hair was gone. She stood before him, shamed and sorrowful, and he grew into a mighty rage. "Who was it did this to you, Sif?" he said. "I am Thor, the strongest of all the Dwellers in Asgard, and I shall see to it that all the powers the Gods possess will be used to get your fairness back. Come with me, Sif." And taking his wife's hand in his, Thor went off to the Council House where the Gods and the Goddesses were.

Sif covered her head with her veil, for she would not have the Gods and Goddesses look upon her shorn head. But from the anger in Thor's eyes all saw that the wrong done to Sif was great indeed. Then Thor told of the cutting of her

Tiny Tricksters

Here are a few of the "little people" making mischief in early European folklore.

- **Dwarfs** lived inside mountains and mines. They usually looked like tiny old men with beards and, sometimes, humped backs. Famous for their metalwork, they were also said to possess secret knowledge.
- **Fairies** were magical little creatures who lived underground or in rock piles. Early fairies were feared for their dangerous powers, but later they were thought of as helpful to humans. Fairies often had green hair and clothes, but they came in many different shapes and types.
- **Pixies** were tiny, mischievous fairies who danced by the light of the moon. Their favorite pranks were leading people astray and frightening children.
- **Goblins** were mean-spirited creatures who lurked in people's homes. At night, they made mischief by banging pots and pans, snatching pajamas, and rearranging furniture.

▲ Thor

beautiful hair. A whisper went round the Council House. "It was Loki did this—no one else in Asgard would have done a deed so shameful," one said to the other.

"Loki it was who did it," said Thor. "He has hidden himself, but I shall find him and I will slay him."

"Nay, not so, Thor," said Odin, the Father of the Gods. "Nay, no Dweller in Asgard may slay another. I shall summon Loki to come before us here. It is for you to make him (and remember that Loki is cunning and able to do many things) bring back to Sif the beauty of her golden hair."

Then the call of Odin, the call that all in Asgard have to harken to, went through the City of the Gods. Loki heard it, and he had to come from his hiding-place and enter the house where the Gods held their Council. And when he looked on Thor and saw the rage that was in his eyes, and when he looked on Odin and saw the sternness in the face of the Father of the Gods, he knew that he would have to make amends for the shameful wrong he had done to Sif.

Said Odin, "There is a thing that you, Loki, have to do: Restore to Sif the beauty of her hair."

Loki looked at Odin, Loki looked at Thor, and he saw that what was said would have to be done. His quick mind searched to find a way of restoring to Sif the beauty of her golden hair.

"I shall do as you command, Odin All-Father," he said.

But before we tell you of what Loki did to restore the beauty of Sif's golden hair, we must tell you of the other beings besides the Gods and the Goddesses who were in the world at the time. First, there was the Vanir. When the Gods who were called the Aesir came to the mountain on which they built Asgard, they found other beings there. These were not wicked and ugly like the Giants; they were beautiful and friendly; the Vanir they were named.

Although they were beautiful and friendly the Vanir had no thought of making the world more beautiful or more happy. In that way they differed from the Aesir who had such a thought. The Aesir made peace with them, and they lived together in friendship, and the Vanir came to do things that helped the Aesir to make the world more beautiful and more happy. Freya,[7] whom the Giant wanted to take away with the Sun and the Moon as a reward for the building of the wall round Asgard, was of the Vanir. The other beings of the Vanir were Frey,[8] who was the brother of Freya, and Niörd, who was their father.

On the earth below there were other beings—the dainty Elves, who danced and fluttered about, attending to the trees and flowers and grasses. The Vanir were permitted to rule over the Elves. Then below the earth, in caves and hollows, there was another race, the Dwarfs or Gnomes, little, twisted creatures, who were both wicked and ugly, but who were the best craftsmen in the world.

In the days when neither the Aesir nor the Vanir were friendly to him Loki used to go down to Svartheim, the Dwarfs' dwelling

---

7. **Freya** (frā'ə): Norse goddess of beauty and love.

8. **Frey** (frā): Norse god of crops, love, prosperity, and peace.

Dwarfs Deliver

No doubt about it—the spear Gungnir and the boat Skidbladnir would come in handy if you were a Norse god. But marvelous as they were, these items weren't the most prized objects ever to be made by the dwarfs. When Loki boasted about these goods, a dwarf named Brock challenged Loki to a wager. He claimed that his brother was the greatest of all master smiths, and that he could produce wonders greater than those gotten by Loki. Loki agreed to the challenge, and together the dwarf brothers set to work. After a time, they presented three objects to the council of the gods—a flying boar, a magical arm-ring, and a hammer by the name of Miölnir. In Thor's hands, this mighty hammer was judged by all the gods the most wondrous of all the dwarfs' works. Loki, as usual, could only hang his head in shame.

below the earth. And now that he was commanded to restore to Sif the beauty of her hair, Loki thought of help he might get from the Dwarfs.

Down, down, through the winding passages in the earth he went, and he came at last to where the Dwarfs who were most friendly to him were working in their forges. All the

Dwarfs were master-smiths, and when he came upon his friends he found them working hammer and tongs, beating metals into many shapes. He watched them for a while and took note of the things they were making. One was a spear, so well balanced and made that it would hit whatever mark it was thrown at no matter how bad the aim the thrower had. The other was a boat that could sail on any sea, but that could be folded up so that it would go into one's pocket. The spear was called Gungnir and the boat was called Skidbladnir.

Loki made himself very agreeable to the Dwarfs, praising their work and promising them things that only the Dwellers in Asgard could give, things that the Dwarfs longed to possess. He talked to them till the little, ugly folk thought that they would come to own Asgard and all that was in it.

At last Loki said to them, "Have you got a bar of fine gold that you can hammer into threads—into threads so fine that they will be like the hair of Sif, Thor's wife? Only the Dwarfs could make a thing so wonderful. Ah, there is the bar of gold. Hammer it into those find threads, and the Gods themselves will be jealous of your work."

Flattered by Loki's speeches, the Dwarfs who were in the forge took up the bar of fine gold and flung it into the fire. Then taking it out and putting it upon their anvil they worked on the bar with their tiny hammers until they beat it into threads that were as fine as the hairs of one's head. But that was not enough. They had to be as fine as the hairs on Sif's head, and these were finer than anything else. They worked on the threads, over and over again, until they were as fine as the hairs on Sif's head. The threads were as bright as sunlight, and when Loki took up the mass of worked gold it flowed from his raised hand down on the ground. It was so fine that it could be put into his palm, and it was so light that a bird might not feel its weight.

Then Loki praised the Dwarfs more and more, and he made more and more promises to them. He charmed them all, although they were an unfriendly and suspicious folk. And before he left them he asked them for the spear and the boat he had seen them make, the spear Gungnir and the boat Skidbladnir. The Dwarfs gave him these things, though in a while after they wondered at themselves for giving them.

Back to Asgard Loki went. He walked into the Council House where the Dwellers in Asgard were gathered. He met the stern look in Odin's eyes and the rageful look in Thor's eyes with smiling good humor. "Off with thy veil, O Sif," he said. And when poor Sif took off her veil he put upon her shorn head the wonderful mass of gold he held in his palm. Over her shoulders the gold fell, fine, soft, and shining as her own hair. And the Aesir and the Asyniur, The Gods and the Goddesses, and the Van and Vana, when they saw Sif's head covered again with the shining web, laughed and clapped their hands in gladness. And the shining web held to Sif's head as if indeed it had roots and was growing there.

▲ Ygdrasil, the great tree in Norse mythology, whose roots and branches hold together the universe.

The Universe of the Norse Gods and Goddesses

There are three levels in the universe of Norse mythology. At the first level, there is Asgard (äs'gärd'), the home of the gods and goddesses. At the middle level, there is Midgard (mid'gärd'), where human beings, dwarfs, and giants live. Niflheim (niv'əl·hām'), the world of the dead, is at the bottom level. All three levels are bound together by the roots and branches of Ygdrasil (ig'drə·sil'), the mighty ash tree.

Here are some of the names that have appeared in the Norse myths in this book. Note that some names may be spelled in more than one way.

Name	Description
Fenris (Fenrir) (fen'ris)	Wolf, the son of Loki
Frey (frā)	god of plenty
Freya (Freyja) (frā'ə)	goddess of love and beauty
Frig (Frigg, Frigga) (frig)	goddess of the heavens; Odin's wife
Heimdall (hām'däl)	watchman of the rainbow bridge
Hel (Hela) (hel)	goddess of the underworld
Jotunheim (Iotunheim) (yô'tʊʊn·hām')	world of the giants
Loki (lō'kē)	god of fire; trickster and sky traveler
Mimir (mē'mir')	guardian of the well of wisdom
Odin (ō'din)	king of the gods and goddesses; god of war, wisdom,and art
Thor (thôr)	lord of thunder
Tyr (tir)	bravest of Aesir gods
Vanir (vä'nir)	nature gods and goddesses who live in Asgard

When confronted with a problem, the trickster often uses oddball logic—or none at all—which causes his scheme to backfire. But when his thinking works, the mischief-maker becomes an instant hero. Read on to see how one American Indian trickster-hero saves the day.

Coyote Kills the Giant

RETOLD BY RICHARD ERDOES AND ALFONSO ORTIZ

Coyote was walking one day when he met Old Woman. She greeted him and asked where he was headed.

"Just roaming around," said Coyote.

"You better stop going that way, or you'll meet a giant who kills everybody."

"Oh, giants don't frighten me," said Coyote (who had never met one).

"I always kill them. I'll fight this one too, and make an end of him."

"He's bigger and closer than you think," said Old Woman.

"I don't care," said Coyote, deciding that a giant would be about as big as a bull moose and calculating that he could kill one easily.

So Coyote said good-bye to Old Woman and went ahead, whistling a tune. On his way he saw a large fallen branch that looked like a club. Picking it up, he said to himself, "I'll hit the giant over the head with this.

You Need to Know...

If you've ever seen him in hot pursuit of the Roadrunner, you know that Wile E. Coyote has plenty of tricks up his sleeve. The coyote in this folk tale is a close cousin of Wile E., although he meets with more success than his cartoon double. The master trickster of Native American lore, Coyote is both clever and comical, a cheater and a savior, a destroyer and a creator. He has a huge appetite and frequently preys upon animals that aren't rightly his. A shape-shifter, Coyote sometimes turns himself into a fish so that he can steal fishhooks and harpoons. Like a clever but mischievous child, Coyote represents creativity in the midst of chaos, freedom in a world full of rules. He may be impossible to control, but this crafty trickster always gives an exhilarating, if dangerous, ride.

It's big enough and heavy enough to kill him." He walked on and came to a huge cave right in the middle of the path. Whistling merrily, he went in.

Suddenly Coyote met a woman who was crawling along on the ground.

"What's the matter?" he asked.

"I'm starving," she said, "and too weak to walk. What are you doing with that stick?"

"I'm going to kill the giant with it," said Coyote, and he asked if she knew where he was hiding.

Feeble as she was, the woman laughed. "You're already in the giant's belly."

"How can I be in his belly?" asked Coyote. "I haven't even met him."

"You probably thought it was a cave when you walked into his mouth," the woman said, and sighed. "It's easy to walk in, but nobody ever walks out. This giant is so big you can't take him in with your eyes. His belly fills a whole valley."

Coyote threw his stick away and kept on walking. What else could he do? Soon he came across some more people lying around half dead. "Are you sick?" he asked.

"No," they said, "just starving to death. We're trapped inside the giant."

"You're foolish," said Coyote. "If we're really inside this giant, then the cave walls must be the inside of his stomach. We can just cut some meat and fat from him."

"We never thought of that," they said.

"You're not as smart as I am," said Coyote.

Coyote took his hunting knife and started cutting chunks out of the cave walls. As he had guessed, they were indeed the giant's fat and meat, and he used it to feed the starving people. He even went back and gave some meat to the

woman he had met first. Then all the people imprisoned in
the giant's belly started to feel stronger and happier, but not
completely happy. "You've fed us," they said, "and thanks.
But how are we going to get out of here?"

"Don't worry," said Coyote. "I'll kill the giant by stabbing
him in the heart. Where is his heart? It must be around here
someplace."

"Look at the volcano puffing and beating over there,"
someone said. "Maybe it's the heart."

"So it is, friend," said Coyote, and began to cut at this
mountain.

Then the giant spoke up. "Is that you, Coyote? I've heard
of you. Stop this stabbing and cutting and let me alone. You
can leave through my mouth; I'll open it for you."

"I'll leave, but not quite yet," said Coyote, hacking at the
heart. He told the others to get ready. "As soon as I have
him in his death throes,[1] there will be an earthquake. He'll

---

1. **throes** (thrōz): struggles.

open his jaw to take a last breath, and then his mouth will close forever. So be ready to run out fast!"

Coyote cut a deep hole in the giant's heart, and lava started to flow out. It was the giant's blood. The giant groaned, and the ground under the people's feet trembled.

"Quick, now!" shouted Coyote. The giant's mouth opened and they all ran out. The last one was the wood tick. The giant's teeth were closing on him, but Coyote managed to pull him through at the last moment.

"Look at me," cried the wood tick, "I'm all flat!"

"It happened when I pulled you through," said Coyote. "You'll always be flat from now on. Be glad you're alive."

"I guess I'll get used to it," said the wood tick, and he did.

Letting Off Steam

This folk tale belongs to the Native American Flathead people of North America. The Flatheads weren't the only people who associated bleeding giants with erupting volcanoes. The ancient Greeks, for example, told a story to explain the creation of Mount Etna, the highest active volcano in Europe. After Zeus and the Olympians conquered the Titans, Mother Earth produced one final, hideous offspring to challenge the victors. Fifty dragons' heads sprang from each shoulder of the giant, and snakes coiled endlessly around his legs. The creature succeeded in wounding and kidnapping Zeus, but the other gods rescued their leader—now bent on revenge. When Zeus let loose his powerful lightning bolts, the giant tried to flee, but was soon overcome. Bleeding, blind, and burning, he sank to the ground, where Zeus pinned him forever in place by dropping a nearby mountain on his chest. It was long believed that when the giant struggled to escape, the earth would quake and the surrounding countryside would be bathed in a fiery flood. In other words, Mount Etna—whose name means "I burn"—would erupt. In the major eruption of 1669, close to 20,000 people sacrificed their lives to the angry giant.

Is bigger always better? In this American folk tale, you'll meet one of the biggest heroes ever to roam the countryside. You'll also see how he gets into—and out of—one very big mess.

Paul Bunyan's Cornstalk

RETOLD BY HAROLD COURLANDER

Paul Bunyan was the fellow who invented the ax with two edges so a man could stand between two trees and chop them both down at the same time. As it turned out, Paul was the only man who could do that trick, but the other lumberjacks used the double-bitted ax anyway, because they didn't have to sharpen the blades so often.

Paul Bunyan also had other tricks. Most lumberjacks used to cut off the tops of the pines before they felled[1] them. But when Paul was in a hurry, he'd wait till a tree started falling; then he'd get set with his ax and lop off the top of the tree as it came down.

Nothing Paul Bunyan ever did was small. He had an ox named Babe, who used to help him with his logging work. Babe was just about the most phenomenal ox in Michigan. His color was blue, and he stood ninety hands high. If you happened to hang on the tip of one horn, it's doubtful if you could have seen

You Need to Know...

The American folk hero Paul Bunyan came to life in the lumber camps of the North during the early 1900s. Bunyan's superhuman size and strength—and his gigantic blue ox, Babe—help him to accomplish incredible feats. According to legend, his camp stove covers an entire acre, and his skillet is so large that it must be greased by men wearing bacon for skates. The stories that tell of Bunyan's capers are known, fittingly, as tall tales. Tall tales are based on wild exaggeration and slapstick humor. They were originally tell-aloud stories of the American frontier, often explaining how lakes, mountains, and rivers were formed or how natural elements such as snow and rain were combated. Although they are rooted in reality, these tales—like Paul Bunyan himself—challenge the imagination to soar to dizzying new heights.

---

1. felled (feld): chopped down.

the tip of the other, even on a clear day. One day when Paul had Babe out plowing, the ox was stung by a Michigan deer fly about the size of a bushel basket. Babe took off across the country dragging the plow behind him, right across Indiana, Illinois, and Missouri, with the deer fly bringing up the rear. After a while Babe veered south and didn't stop till he got to the Rio Grande. The plow that Babe was hitched to dug a furrow four miles wide and two hundred miles long. You can check it in your own geography book. They call it Grand Canyon nowadays.

Even the storms that Paul was in were big. The biggest of all was the one they call the Big Blue Snow. It snowed for two months straight, and the way the drifts piled up only the tops of the tallest pines were showing. Lumberjacks went out that winter on their snowshoes and cut off all the pine tops. It saved them a lot of time when spring came around. Babe the blue ox didn't get a wink of sleep, though, from December till the first of March. It seems that standing out there in the weather the way he was, the snow that fell on his back melted and ran down his tail, and once it got there it froze into ice. Babe's tail kept getting heavier and heavier, and it drew on his side so hard it just pulled his

▲ Statues of Paul Bunyan, standing 49 feet tall, and Babe in Klamath, California.

eyelids wide open and kept them that way. Babe never did get his eyes closed until the spring thaw came and melted the ice off his tail.

But the Big Blue Snow wasn't anything compared to the big drouth[2] that started in Saginaw County and spread out as far as the Alleghenies in the East and the Rockies in the West. It all started with Paul Bunyan's vegetable garden. Paul planted some corn and some pumpkins. One of those cornstalks was six feet high before the others had sprouted. In two weeks it was tall as a house and growing like crazy. About the time it was as big as a fifty-year-old pine, people began to come in from all over the county to see it. It was growing out of the ground so fast it was pulling up stones that even the frost couldn't heave out. Same kind of thing, more or less, happened to one of the pumpkin vines. It grew so fast it just darted around like a Massauga rattlesnake. It climbed into any place where there was an opening. People had to keep their windows closed. The ones that didn't had to cut their way out of their beds with a brush knife. Sometimes that vine would grow into one window and out another between sunset and sunrise. Things weren't too bad until the vine blossomed and the pumpkins came out. They were about the size of hogsheads[3]—the little pumpkins, that is—and when the vine whipped back and forth looking for some-place to grow it just snapped the pumpkins around like crab apples on a string. People had to be mighty alert to keep from getting hit by those pumpkins. One man lost a

---

2. **drouth** (drouth): a long period with no rain (also spelled drought).

3. **hogsheads** (hôgz'hedz'): large barrels.

team of horses that way, and half a dozen good barns and one silo were stoved in.

But the real problem started when the corn and pumpkin roots began to soak up all the water out of the ground. Farms for sixty miles around went dry—fields, springs, and wells. The pine woods turned yellow from lack of moisture. The Au Sable River just turned into a trickle, and pretty soon there wasn't anything there but dry mud. The next thing that happened was that the water in the Great Lakes began to go down. It went down so fast in Lake Huron it left the fish hanging in the air. When things began to look real bad, folks came and told Paul Bunyan he'd just have to get rid of his corn and pumpkins. Paul was reasonable about it. First he went after the pumpkin vine. He spent four hours racing around trying to catch hold of the end, and finally did it by trapping it in a barn. He hitched Babe up to the end of the vine, but as fast as Babe pulled the vine grew. Babe ran faster and faster, and he was near Lake Ontario before he had the vine tight enough to pull it out.

Then Paul sized up his corn-stalk. He figured he'd have to chop it down. He sharpened up his ax and spit on his hands. He made a good deep cut in that stalk, but before he could chip out a wedge the stalk grew up six feet, cut and all. Every time he

Dream Team

Paul Bunyan wasn't the only larger-than-life American folk hero. Here's a brief introduction to a few of Bunyan's legendary buddies.

- **Daniel Boone,** unlike Bunyan, was a real person. In the 1700s, he helped blaze a trail through the Appalachian Mountains. Although he never wore a coonskin cap, he did dress in deerskin leggings and moccasins. His rifle, Tick-Licker, was his constant companion.

- **John Henry** is the African American hero of a folk song about a worker who lived in the 1870s. In the song—and perhaps in real life—a railroad worker by this name competed against a steam drill to prove that a man with a hammer could dig a hole faster. He won the contest, but died on the spot from exhaustion.

- **Pecos Bill** is the Paul Bunyan of the Southwest. This exaggerated cowboy was said to have been raised by coyotes in Texas. He used a rattle-snake as a lasso, taught broncos how to buck, rode a tornado without a saddle, and suppos-edly laughed himself to death when asked silly questions about the West by an easterner.

made a cut it would shoot up out of reach before he could swing his ax again. Pretty soon he saw there wasn't any use going on this way. "Only way to kill this stalk is to cut off the top," he said. He hung his ax in his belt and started climbing. In about two hours he was completely out of sight. People just stood around and waited. They stood around two and a half days without any sight of Paul. Lars Larson called, "Paul!" but there was no answer. Erik Erikson and Hans Hanson called, "Paul!" But there wasn't any word from Paul Bunyan. So they waited some more. Two more days went by. No word from Paul. They decided that if everyone yelled at once maybe the sound would carry. So all together the two thousand eight hundred men and boys hollered, "Paul!" And sure enough, they heard his faint voice from up above.

"When you going to top that cornstalk?" they yelled back at him.

"Hasn't that top come down yet?" Paul hollered back. "I cut it off three days ago!"

And it was the truth, too. The stalk stopped growing, the water in the Great Lakes stopped falling, the Au Sable River began to run, the springs began to flow again, and things came back to normal. But it was a narrow escape.

Is fame a matter of luck, or cleverness? What would you do to have your name known by all? In this African folk tale, the trickster Ananse must overcome his fears to secure the fame he seeks.

Spider's Bargain with God

TRANSLATED BY JACK BERRY

Kwaku Ananse, the spider, went to Sky God Nana Nyamee and asked whether he could buy the stories told about Him so they would be told about Ananse instead. Nana Nyamee said, "Yes, provided you bring me the following things in payment."

Ananse said, "I am willing. Just name them."

Nana Nyamee said, "Bring me a live leopard, a pot full of live bees, and a live python." Ananse was afraid, but nevertheless he agreed to provide them. He went home and sat down and thought and thought.

At last he took a needle and thread, and set out toward the forest where the leopard lived. When he got to the stream where Leopard got his water, he sat down, took out the needle and thread, and sewed his eye-lids together. He waited. When he heard the footsteps of Leopard coming to fetch water, he began to sing to himself: "Hmm. Nana Nyamee is wonderful. He sewed my eyes and took me to his palace. Then I began to see wonderful things, and I have been singing of them ever since. Beautiful

> **You Need to Know...**
> This folk tale about the spider-trickster Ananse belongs to the Ashanti people of West Africa. There, the stories Ananse wants to buy from the sky god are called *Anansesem,* or spider tales. Ananse is only one of several tricksters from Africa. The tortoise and the hare also entertain audiences with their clever pranks. Whatever form the trickster takes, these tales are the most popular of all tell-aloud stories. Today most of these kinds of stories have been written down, but for hundreds of years they existed only in the mouths of their tellers—who, like Ananse himself, have spun clever story threads across countless generations.

women, palaces, rich and delicious food, and a wonderful life."

Leopard came up to him and asked Ananse, "What were you singing about?"

He replied, "Hmm. Nana Nyamee is wonderful. He sewed my eyes and took me to his palace. Then I began to see wonderful things, and I have been singing of them ever since. Beautiful women, palaces, rich and delicious food, and a wonderful life."

Leopard said, "Eh, Ananse, what is it, are you dreaming?" "No," said Ananse, "there is a beautiful woman here."

Leopard said, "Please Ananse, sew my eyes shut, too, and lead me to Nana Nyamee so that I, too, may see all the wonderful things."

"No, I know you, Leopard, when you see her and all those other beautiful creatures you will kill them and eat them up."

"No, No, No," Leopard growled. "I shall not. Rather, I shall thank you."

Ananse took his needle and thread and sewed Leopard's eyes and led him to Nana Nyamee's palace. He said, "Nana Nyamee, here is the first installment. Keep it."

Next day Ananse took an earthenware pot and went to a place where he knew there were honey bees. As he came near the place he sang, "Oh bees! Oh bees!"

The bees said, "Ananse, what is all this murmuring about?"

Ananse replied, "I have had an argument with Nana Nyamee. He says all of you together won't fill this pot, but I say you will, and so I came to find out."

They said, "Oho, that is easy," and they flew into the pot, buzz, buzz, buzz, until the pot was full, and every bee had flown into it. Then Ananse quickly sealed the pot and carried it off to Nana Nyamee as his second installment.

For two days he could not think how to get the third—a live python. But at last he hit on a plan. He went to the forest and cut a long stick, a stick as long as a tree. He carried this off to the forest, singing to himself, "I am right, he is wrong! He is wrong, I am right."

When Python saw him he said, "Ananse, what are you grumbling about?"

He answered, "How lucky I am to meet you here. I have had a long and bitter argument with Nana Nyamee. I have known you for a long time, and I know your measurements both when you are coiled, and when you are fully stretched out. Nana Nyamee thinks very little of you. He thinks you are only a little longer than the green mamba, and no longer than the cobra. I strongly disagree with him, and to prove my point I brought this pole to measure you."

Python was very angry, and he began stretching himself out to his greatest length along the stick.

And Ananse said, "You are moving! You are moving! Let me tie you to the stick so I can get the measurement exactly right."

And Python agreed. As Ananse tied Python up he sang a little song, and when he had Python securely fastened to the stick, Ananse carried him off to Nana Nyamee.

Nana Nyamee was very pleased with Ananse and forthwith beat the gong throughout the world that all stories should be told about Ananse.

This is how Ananse became the leading figure in all Ananse stories.

Hiss-story

The python is a large snake native to Asia, India, Australia, and Africa. African pythons can grow up to thirty feet long. Like boas, pythons are constrictors; they kill their victims by squeezing them to death. A monster serpent in Greek mythology, Python, gave the snake its name. The spot on which Apollo slew this serpent became known as Pytho, later the town of Delphi. People would travel to this place to hear oracles, or predictions, from a priestess known as the "pythoness." Likewise, the athletic games that were held there every four years were originally called the Pythian games.

Have you ever started off on an ordinary journey and ended up having an extraordinary adventure? In this fairy tale, you will meet a young man whose unselfish choices lead him into a world of wonder and joy.

The Golden Goose

JAKOB AND WILHELM GRIMM

There was once a man who had three sons. The youngest of them was called Dullhead, and was sneered and jeered at and snubbed on every possible opportunity.

One day it happened that the eldest son wished to go into the forest to cut wood, and before he started his mother gave him a fine rich cake and a bottle of wine, so that he might be sure not to suffer from hunger or thirst.

When he reached the forest he met a little old gray man who wished him "Good-morning," and said, "Do give me a piece of that cake you have got in your pocket, and let me have a draft[1] of your wine—I am so hungry and thirsty."

But this clever son replied, "If I give you my cake and wine I shall have none left for myself; you just go your own way;" and he left the little man standing there and went further on into the forest. There he began to cut

---

You Need to Know...

What does "The Golden Goose" have in common with "Hansel and Gretel," "Snow White," and "Little Red Riding Hood"? Along with dozens of others, these fairy tales were all recorded in the early 1800s by two German brothers, Jacob and Wilhelm Grimm. During this time in Germany, the middle and working classes were growing more and more unhappy, and the government was coming under attack. The Grimm brothers believed that by collecting and spreading the stories of the common folk—the woodcutters, the cowherds, and the farmers—they could stir a sense of pride in their folk traditions. The Grimms' collection of fairy tales, *Nursery and Household Tales,* contained some two hundred stories from all over Europe. A popular work even today, this collection has, in fact, helped to keep the spirit of these folk heroes alive.

---

1. **draft** (draft): drink.

down a tree, but before long he made a false stroke with his axe, and cut his own arm so badly that he was obliged to go home and have it bound up.

Then the second son went to the forest, and his mother gave him a good cake and a bottle of wine as she had to his elder brother. He too met the little old gray man, who begged him for a morsel[2] of cake and a draft of wine.

But the second son spoke most sensibly too, and said, "Whatever I give to you I deprive myself of. Just go your own way, will you?" Not long after his punishment over-took him, for no sooner had he struck a couple of blows on a tree with his axe, than he cut his leg so badly that he had to be carried home.

So then Dullhead said, "Father, let me go out and cut wood."

But his father answered, "Both your brothers have injured themselves. You had better leave it alone; you know nothing about it."

---

2. **morsel** (môr'səl): small bite.

Mother Goose Mystery

Perhaps the most famous goose in the world of children's literature is Mother Goose. Famous as she is, though, no one is sure whether she ever really exist-ed. Some scholars think the original Mother Goose lived in the eighth century A.D. This woman, known as "Goose-Footed Bertha," was the mother of the powerful ruler Charlemagne. She was also a great friend and helper of children. Other scholars trace Mother Goose to a woman named Elizabeth Goose (or possibly Vergoose) who lived in Boston during Colonial times. She entertained her grandchildren with lively tales and rhymes that were supposedly published in 1719. However, no copy of this book has ever been discovered. In fact, the first Mother Goose books seem to have come to America from Europe in the late 1700s. Some of these collections pictured Mother Goose as an old woman with a crooked nose; others showed a woman with a pointed hat and a magic wand, flying on the back of a goose. Like the stories she told, she may forever remain a legend.

But Dullhead begged so hard to be allowed to go that at last his father said, "Very well, then—go. Perhaps when you have hurt yourself, you may learn to know better." His mother only gave him a very plain cake made with water and baked in the cinders, and a bottle of sour beer.

When he got to the forest, he too met the little gray old man, who greeted him and said, "Give me a piece of your cake and a draft from your bottle; I am so hungry and thirsty."

And Dullhead replied, "I've only got a cinder-cake and some sour beer, but if you care to have that, let us sit down and eat."

So they sat down, and when Dullhead brought out his cake he found it had turned into a fine rich cake, and the sour beer into excellent wine. Then they ate and drank, and when they had finished the little man said, "Now I will bring you luck, because you have a kind heart and are willing to share what you have with others. There stands an old tree; cut it down, and among its roots you'll find something." With that the little man took leave.

Then Dullhead fell to at once to hew down the tree, and when it fell he found among its roots a goose, whose feathers were all of pure gold. He lifted it out, carried it off, and took it with him to an inn where he meant to spend the night.

Now the landlord of the inn had three daughters, and when they saw the goose they were filled with curiosity as to what this wonderful bird could be, and each longed to have one of its golden feathers.

The eldest thought to herself, "No doubt I shall soon find a good opportunity to pluck out one of its feathers," and the first time Dullhead happened to leave the room she caught hold of the goose by its wing. But, lo and behold! her fingers seemed to stick fast to the goose, and she could not take her hand away.

Soon after the second daughter came in, and thought to pluck a golden feather for herself too; but hardly had she touched her sister than she stuck fast as well. At last the third sister came with the same intentions, but the other two cried out, "Keep off! for Heaven's sake, keep off!"

The younger sister could not imagine why she was to keep off, and thought to herself, "If they are both there, why should not I be there too?"

So she sprang to them; but no sooner had she touched one of them than she stuck fast to her. So they all three had to spend the night with the goose.

Next morning Dullhead tucked the goose under his arm and went off, without in the least troubling himself about the three girls who were hanging on to it. They just had to run after him right or left as best they could. In the middle of a field they met the parson,[3] and when he saw this

---

3. **parson** (pär'sən): minister of a church.

Magical Helper

In fairy tales, heroes often have magical helpers to thank—wizards, magicians, or fairies who offer timely assistance. These helpers might reward a common person for good behavior, as in the fairy tale you are reading. They also enjoy rescuing the downtrodden—those who are ugly, dull-witted, or mistreated by others. Cinderella's fairy godmother, for example, saves the suffering girl by transforming her into a ballroom beauty. Other magical helpers seek to boost a talented young person into the ranks of the heroic. The magician Merlin educates the young Arthur and advises him during his reign as king, for instance, and Yoda trains Luke Skywalker to use The Force. What other magical helpers can you pull from your hat?

procession he cried, "For shame, you bold girls! What do you mean by running after a young fellow through the fields like that? Do you call that proper behavior?" And with that he caught the youngest girl by the hand to try and draw her away. But directly he touched her he hung on himself, and had to run along with the rest of them.

Not long after the clerk came that way, and was much surprised to see the parson following the footsteps of three girls. "Why, where is your reverence going so fast?" cried he; "don't forget there is to be a christening[4] today," and he ran after him, caught him by the sleeve, and hung on to it himself. As the five of them trotted along in this fashion one after the other, two peasants were coming from their work

---

4. christening (kris'ən•iŋ): baptism.

with their hoes. On seeing them the parson called out and begged them to come and rescue him and the clerk. But no sooner did they touch the clerk than they stuck on too, and so there were seven of them running after Dullhead and his goose.

After a time they all came to a town where a King reigned whose daughter was so serious and solemn that no one could ever manage to make her laugh. So the King had decreed[5] that whoever should succeed in making her laugh should marry her.

When Dullhead heard this he marched before the Princess with his goose and its appendages,[6] and as soon as she saw these seven people continually running after each other she burst out laughing, and could not stop herself. Then Dullhead claimed her as his bride, but the King, who did not much fancy him as a son-in-law, made all sorts of objections, and told him he must first find a man who could drink up a whole cellarful of wine.

Dullhead thought of the little gray man, who could, he felt sure, help him; so he went off to the forest, and on the very spot where he had cut down the tree he saw a man sitting with a most dismal expression on his face.

Dullhead asked him what he was taking so much to heart, and the man answered, "I don't know how I am ever to quench[7] this terrible thirst I am suffering from. Cold water doesn't suit me at all. To be sure I've emptied a whole barrel of wine, but what is one drop on a hot stone?"

"I think I can help you," said Dullhead. "Come with me, and you shall drink to your heart's content." So he took him to the King's cellar, and the man sat down before the huge

---

5. **decreed** (dē·krēd'): officially ordered.

6. **appendages** (ə·pen'dij·əz'): anything attached to something else.

7. **quench** (kwench): satisfy.

casks[8] and drank and drank till he drank up the whole contents of the cellar before the day closed.[9]

Then Dullhead asked once more for his bride, but the King felt vexed[10] at the idea of a stupid fellow whom people called Dullhead carrying off his daughter, and he began to make fresh conditions. He required Dullhead to find a man who could eat a mountain of bread. Dullhead did not wait to consider long but went straight off to the forest, and there on the same spot sat a man who was drawing in a strap as tight as he could round his body, and making a most woeful[11] face the while. Said he, "I've eaten up a whole oven full of loaves, but what's the good of that to anyone who is as hungry as I am? I declare my stomach feels quite empty, and I must draw my belt tight if I'm not to die of starvation."

Dullhead was delighted, and said, "Get up and come with me, and you shall have plenty to eat," and he brought him to the King's Court.

Now the King had given orders to have all the flour in his kingdom brought together, and to have

Goofy Goose Facts

The goose is not as glamorous as the swan, nor as beloved as the duck. But this brownish gray water bird was honored in many cultures. Here are a few facts and bits of folk wisdom concerning these feathery fowl.

- Geese honk—until their young are disturbed. When this happens, they hiss angrily. They also attack the intruder with their jabbing bills and flapping wings.
- Geese can fly for 1,000 miles or more without stopping to rest!
- Geese were kept by the ancient Greeks and Romans in their temples as guards.
- In Egyptian mythology, the Nile Goose was the creator of the world.
- In Asia, the goose is regarded as the Bird of Heaven and bearer of good tidings.
- If the goose honks high, the weather will be fair; if it honks low, the weather will be foul.

---

8. **casks** (kaskz): barrels for holding liquids.

9. **closed** (klozd): ended.

10. **vexed** (vekst): upset.

11. **woeful** (wō'fəl): sad.

a huge mountain baked of it. But the man from the wood just took up his stand before the mountain and began to eat, and in one day it had all vanished.

For the third time Dullhead asked for his bride, but again the King tried to make some evasion,[12] and demanded a ship "which could sail on land or water! When you come sailing in such a ship," said he, "you shall have my daughter without further delay."

Again Dullhead started off to the forest, and there he found the little old gray man with whom he had shared his cake, and who said, "I have eaten and I have drunk for you, and now I will give you the ship. I have done all this for you because you were kind and merciful to me."

Then he gave Dullhead a ship which could sail on land or water, and when the King saw it he felt he could no longer refuse him his daughter.

So they celebrated the wedding with great rejoicings; and after the King's death Dullhead succeeded to the kingdom, and lived happily with his wife for many years after.

---

12. **evasion** (ē•vā'zhən): way of avoiding an obligation.

Read On

Two collections that will give you more folk and fairy tales are *Favorite Folktales from Around the World* by Jane Yolen (Pantheon) and *The Complete Fairy Tales of the Brothers Grimm* by Jack Zipes (Bantam). Two novels with fairy tale themes are *Goose Chase* by Patrice Kindl (Houghton Mifflin) and *Ella Enchanted* by Gail Carson Levine (HarperTrophy).

Have you ever wondered what an animal or object might say if it could talk? In this African folk tale, several unsuspecting men find out and wish they hadn't.

Talk

HAROLD COURLANDER AND GEORGE HERZOG

Once, not far from the city of Accra[1] on the Gulf of Guinea,[2] a country man went out to his garden to dig up some yams to take to market. While he was digging, one of the yams said to him:

"Well, at last you're here. You never weeded me, but now you come around with your digging stick. Go away and leave me alone!"

The farmer turned around and looked at his cow in amazement. The cow was chewing her cud and looking at him.

"Did you say something?" he asked.

The cow kept on chewing and said nothing, but the man's dog spoke up.

"It wasn't the cow who spoke to you," the dog said. "It was the yam. The yam says leave him alone."

The man became angry, because his dog had never

You Need to Know...

This folk tale comes from the Ashanti people of Ghana, in West Africa. (For another Ashanti tale, see "Spider's Bargain with God" on page 193.) The characters in this story busy themselves with some of the most common jobs in Ghana: farming, fishing, and weaving. About the time when Columbus was landing in the Americas, Ghana's rich natural resources—including gold—also drew explorers and traders from Europe. By the mid-1800s, Ghana was under British rule and dubbed the Gold Coast Colony. The Ashanti kept their strong traditions alive, and in 1957 Ghana won its independence. "Talk," with its charming characters, fast-paced action, and absurd humor, reflects the lively imagination of the Ashanti culture and its storytellers.

---

1. **Accra** (ə•krä'): city in Africa; capital of Ghana.
2. **Gulf of Guinea** (gin'ē): inlet of the Atlantic Ocean on the west central coast of Africa.

talked before, and he didn't like his tone besides. So he took his knife and cut a branch from a palm tree to whip his dog. Just then the palm tree said:

"Put that branch down!"

The man was getting very upset about the way things were going, and he started to throw the palm branch away, but the palm branch said:

"Man, put me down softly!"

He put the branch down gently on a stone, and the stone said:

"Hey, take that thing off me!"

This was enough, and the frightened farmer started to run for his village. On the way he met a fisherman going the other way with a fish trap on his head.

"What's the hurry?" the fisherman asked.

"My yam said, 'Leave me alone!' Then the dog said, 'Listen to what the yam says!' When I went to whip the dog with a palm branch the tree said, 'Put that branch down!' Then the palm branch said, 'Do it softly!' Then the stone said, 'Take that thing off me!'"

"Is that all?" the man with the fish trap asked. "Is that so frightening?"

"Well," the man's fish trap said, "did he take it off the stone?"

"Wah!" the fisherman shouted. He threw the fish trap on the ground and began to run with the farmer, and on the trail they met a weaver with a bundle of cloth on his head.

"Where are you going in such a rush?" he asked them.

"My yam said, 'Leave me alone!'" the farmer said. "The dog said, 'Listen to what the yam says!' The tree said, 'Put that branch down!' The branch said, 'Do it softly!' And the stone said, 'Take that thing off me!'"

"And then," the fisherman continued, "the fish trap said, 'Did he take it off?'"

"That's nothing to get excited about," the weaver said, "no reason at all."

"Oh yes it is," his bundle of cloth said. "If it happened to you you'd run too!"

"Wah!" the weaver shouted. He threw his bundle on the trail and started running with the other men.

They came panting to the ford in the river and found a man bathing.

"Are you chasing a gazelle?" he asked them.

The first man said breathlessly:

"My yam talked at me, and it said, 'Leave me alone!' And my dog said, 'Listen to your yam!' And when I cut myself a branch the tree said, 'Put that branch down!' And the branch said, 'Do it softly!' And the stone said, 'Take that thing off me!'"

The fisherman panted:

"And my trap said, 'Did he?'"

The weaver wheezed:

"And my bundle of cloth said, 'You'd run too!'"

"Is that why you're running?" the man in the river asked.

"Well, wouldn't you run if you were in their position?" the river said.

The man jumped out of the water and began to run with the others. They ran down the main street of the village to the house of the chief. The chief's servants brought his stool out, and he came and sat on it to listen to their complaints. The men began to recite their troubles.

"I went out to my garden to dig yams," the farmer said, waving his arms. "Then everything began to talk! My yam said, 'Leave me alone!' My dog said, 'Pay attention to your yam!' The tree said, 'Put that branch down!' The branch said, 'Do it softly!' And the stone said, 'Take it off me!'"

"And my fish trap said, 'Well, did he take it off?'" the fisherman said.

"And my cloth said, 'You'd run too!'" the weaver said.

"And the river said the same," the bather said hoarsely, his eyes bulging.

The chief listened to them patiently, but he couldn't refrain from scowling.

"Now this is really a wild story," he said at last. "You'd better all go back to your work before I punish you for disturbing the peace."

So the men went away, and the chief shook his head and mumbled to himself, "Nonsense like that upsets the community."

"Fantastic, isn't it?" his stool said. "Imagine, a talking yam!"

The Talking Stool

Animals and objects often talk in African folk tales. In this one, however, the gift of gab is seen as unusual, even frightening. This is done for a specific purpose. By making the characters skittish and chasing them all the way to the tribal chief, the storyteller is able to set up the story's punch line—the chief's talking stool. While native Africans greatly respect their chiefs and leaders, they are also ready and willing to poke fun at their seriousness. To make the chief's stool talk is a good way to do this. In West Africa, such stools are beautiful artworks, carved in painstaking detail by experienced craftspeople. Much like European thrones, these stools are used only by the king or the chief. They symbolize his power, his stability, and his readiness to perform kingly duties. To make such a stool talk, especially in a sassy manner, is to turn the stool against the chief. This calls into question the chief's power and wisdom—and gives the common folk a powerful laugh.

The best riddles and jokes contain a good deal of wisdom. They force us to think differently than we usually do—to appreciate the contradictions in life and to set aside, at least briefly, our logical view of the world.

The Alternative

IDRIES SHAH

"I am a hospitable man," said Nasrudin to a group of cronies at the teahouse. "Very well, then—take us all home to supper," said the greediest.

Nasrudin collected the whole crowd and started towards his house with them.

When he was almost there, he said:

"I'll go ahead and warn my wife: you just wait here."

His wife cuffed him when he told her the news. "There is no food in the house—turn them away."

"I can't do that, my reputation for hospitality is at stake."

"Very well, you go upstairs and I'll tell them that you are out."

After nearly an hour the guests became restless and crowded round the door, shouting, "Let us in, Nasrudin."

The Mulla's wife went out to them.

"Nasrudin is out."

"But we saw him go into the house, and we have been watching the door all the time."

You Need to Know...

The jokester Mulla Nasrudin has mysterious origins. His words of wit and wisdom can be found in many different cultures, from France, Greece, and Turkey, to the Middle East, Russia, and China. He is so popular that many nations claim him as their own. The Turks, for example, have set up a grave for this legendary character and marked it with the date of his supposed death, A.D. 386. However, Nasrudin is quite impossible to pin down. He is both logical and illogical, stupid and clever, blind and all-seeing. His quips and questions are famous for their absurd humor and are often used simply to make people laugh. But they carry a deeper meaning. Many people use them to gain access to a higher wisdom, one that lies beyond rigid, everyday thinking. "I am upside down in this life," Nasrudin is reported to have said. By listening carefully to his words, we, too, can enjoy a momentary mental somersault.

She was silent.

The Mulla, watching from an upstairs window, was unable to contain himself. Leaning out he shouted: "I could have gone out by the back door, couldn't I?"

See what I mean?

IDRIES SHAH

Nasrudin was throwing handfuls of crumbs around his house. "What are you doing?" someone asked him.

"Keeping the tigers away."

"But there are no tigers in these parts."

"That's right. Effective, isn't it?"

There is more Light here

IDRIES SHAH

Someone saw Nasrudin searching for something on the ground. "What have you lost, Mulla?" he asked. "My key," said the Mulla. So they both went down on their knees and looked for it.

After a time the other man asked: "Where exactly did you drop it?"

"In my own house."

"Then why are you looking here?"

"There is more light here than inside my own house."

▲ *Mulla* is a respectful title for an educated Muslim man. In these wisdom tales, Nasrudin is called "Mulla." In what sense is he both foolish and wise?

The following stories were first told over 2,500 years ago—but they still hold important lessons for people today. As you read, ask yourself what human qualities the stories focus on.

The Fox and the Crow

AESOP

One bright morning as the Fox was following his sharp nose through the wood in search of a bite to eat, he saw a Crow on the limb of a tree overhead. This was by no means the first Crow the Fox had ever seen. What caught his attention this time and made him stop for a second look, was that the lucky Crow held a bit of cheese in her beak.

"No need to search any farther," thought sly Master Fox. "Here is a dainty bite for my breakfast."

Up he trotted to the foot of the tree in which the Crow was sitting, and looking up admiringly, he cried, "Good-morning, beautiful creature!"

The Crow, her head cocked on one side, watched the Fox suspiciously. But she kept her beak tightly closed on the cheese and did not return his greeting.

"What a charming creature she is!" said the Fox. "How her feathers shine! What a beautiful form and what splendid wings! Such a wonderful Bird should have a very lovely voice, since everything else about her is so perfect. Could she sing just one song, I know I should hail her Queen of Birds."

> **You Need to Know...**
> Stories such as these are known as fables. A fable is a short, simple tale that teaches a lesson, or a moral. Unlike a myth, a fable does not try to explain the behavior of nature or the gods. Instead, its purpose is to show *humans* how they should behave. Fables often include animal characters who think and talk like human beings. Fable tellers hope that their listeners will see themselves in these animals and avoid the animals' mistakes. Many ancient fables are attributed to a man named Aesop. Aesop is thought to have been an African who was enslaved in Greece and lived during the sixth century B.C. The many fables of the ancient world have been collected under his name for centuries.

Listening to these flattering words, the Crow forgot all her suspicion, and also her breakfast. She wanted very much to be called Queen of Birds.

So she opened her beak wide to utter her loudest caw, and down fell the cheese straight into the Fox's open mouth.

"Thank you," said Master Fox sweetly, as he walked off. "Though it is cracked, you have a voice sure enough. But where are your wits?"

The flatterer lives at the expense of those who will listen to him.

The Wolf in Sheep's Clothing

AESOP

A certain Wolf could not get enough to eat because of the watchfulness of the Shepherds. But one night he found a sheep skin that had been cast aside and forgotten. The next day, dressed in the skin, the Wolf strolled into the pasture with the Sheep. Soon a little Lamb was following him about and was quickly led away to slaughter.

That evening the Wolf entered the fold with the flock. But it happened that the Shepherd took a fancy for mutton broth that very evening, and, picking up a knife, went to the fold. There the first he laid hands on and killed was the Wolf.

The evildoer often comes to harm through his own deceit.

This fable is one of many *Jatakas*, stories belonging to the Buddhist tradition. Buddha had been born into many lives before he became a great spiritual teacher. During his life as the Buddha, he told hundreds of these *Jatakas*, or fables, that grew out of the wisdom he had gained in these lives.

THE LITTLE GRAY DONKEY

DEMI

Once upon a time, there was a merchant who carried his goods on the back of a donkey. At the end of each day he would look for some rich fields of barley and rice. Then, when no one was looking, he would throw a lion skin over the donkey, turn him loose, and let him eat to his heart's content. When farmers saw this creature in the twilight, they thought he was a lion and didn't dare come near him! The merchant became cocky. He thought, I sell to the people by day, and I rob them by night. I am so tricky! I am so smart!

One sunny day, as the merchant was having breakfast, he let his donkey loose in a rich barley field with the lion skin on. These farmers are so stupid, they won't know the difference between day and night, he thought.

The farmers did think it was the lion again, but this time they summoned all the other villagers, who descended on the field waving hoes and rakes and beating drums and gongs. The donkey was scared out of his wits! He gasped and brayed, "Hee-haw! Hee-haw! Hee-haw! Hee-haw!" and the lion skin fell off his back. When the farmers saw it was only a donkey, they roared with laughter. They chased him away with hoes and rakes and beating drums. And they chased his master away, as well.

Don't be deceived by a donkey in a lion's skin.

Glossary

The glossary below is an alphabetical list of words that may be unfamiliar to readers of this book. Some names and more obsure words in this book are not listed here, but instead are defined for you in the footnotes that accompany many of the selections.

Many words in the English language have more than one meaning. This glossary gives the meanings that apply to the words as they are used in the selections in this book.

Each word's pronunciation is given in parentheses. A guide to the pronunciation symbols appears at the bottom of this page.

The following abbreviations are used:

adj. adjective   *adv.* adverb   *n.* noun   *v.* verb

abandon (ə•ban'dən) *v.:* to give up wholly; to leave, desert.

abandoned (ə•ban'dənd) *adj.:* left empty; deserted or unused.

abyss (ə•bis') *n.:* a space so deep it cannot be measured.

adversary (ad'vər•ser'ē) *n.:* an enemy; an opponent.

amends (ə•mendz') *n.:* something done or given to make up for a wrong or a loss.

anguish (aŋ'gwish) *n.:* great pain of mind or body; agony.

appease (ə•pēz') *v.:* satisfy; pacify.

appointed (ə•point'id) *adj.:* officially selected; named.

archenemies (ärch'en'ə•mēz) *n.:* major enemies.

arrest (ə•rest') *v.:* to stop.

ashen (ash'ən) *adj.:* gray as the color of ashes; pale.

asunder (ə•sun'dər) *adv.:* into separate parts.

avails (ə•vālz') *v.:* helps; is of use.

avenged (ə•venjd') *v.:* took revenge for.

bade (bad) *v.:* commanded; ordered.

bedraggled (bē•drag'əld) *adj.:* wet, dirty, and messy, as by dragging through the mud.

biers (birz) *n.:* stands on which coffins or corpses are placed.

bloated (blōt'id) *adj.:* swollen; puffed up.

bolsters (bōl'stərz) *n.:* long pillows.

borne (bôrn) *v.:* tolerated; stood.

boughs (bouz) *n.:* large tree branches.

bridle (brīd''l) *n.:* a head harness used for controlling a horse.

broke (brōk) *v.:* came to an end; stopped.

cherished (cher'isht) *v.:* held affection for; treated tenderly.

cleft (kleft) *n.:* a crack or opening.

cocky (käk'ē) *adj.:* being too sure of oneself; conceited.

composed (kəm•pōzd') *v.:* formed; made up.

contours (kän'toōrz') *n.:* outlines of shapes or forms.

convened (kən•vēnd') *v.:* called together; summoned to meet.

coronet (kôr'ə•net') *n.:* a small crown worn by people of high rank.

council (koun'səl) *n.:* a group called for discussion or decision making.

countenance (koun'tə•nəns) *n.:* face.

course (kôrs) *n.:* a path or direction of motion.

crony (krō'nē) *n.:* old friend.

cuff (kuf) *v.:* to slap or to hit.

decked (dekt) *v.:* dressed or covered in a fine way.

decreed (dē•krēd') *v.:* ordered or decided; proclaimed.

denounces (dē•nouns'iz) *v.:* speaks openly against; condemns.

derision (di•rizh'ən) *n.:* ridicule; scorn.

diadem (dī'ə•dem') *n.:* crown.

dint (dint) *n.:* force.

dirge (durj) *n.:* mournful, slow song.

disarray (dis'ə•rā') *n.:* a state of disorder or confusion.

discus (dis'kəs) *n.:* a heavy disc, usually made of metal and wood, that is thrown for distance in an athletic event.

dissuade (di•swād') *v.:* to persuade or advise against an action.

divinities (də•vin'ə•tēz) *n.:* divine beings; gods.

downy (dou'nē) *adj.:* soft and fluffy.

excel (ek•sel') *v.:* to be better than.

festooned (fes•toōnd') *v.:* hung with flowers, leaves, colored paper, or other material.

forge (fôrj) *n.:* location where metal is heated and hammered into shape.

forlorn (fôr•lôrn') *adj.:* sad and lonely.

fouled (fould) *v.:* made dirty or rotten.

gait (gāt) *n.:* a way of running or walking.

garland (gär'lənd) *n.:* wreath or woven rope.

---

a *as in* cat; ā *as in* day; ä *as in* lot; e *as in* hen; ē *as in* me; i *as in* win; ī *as in* sky; ō *as in* grow; ô *as in* ball; oo *as in* book; ōō *as in* new; yoo *as in* your; yōō *as in* you; oi *as in* joy; ou *as in* now; u *as in* what; ʉ *as in* sure; ə *as in* ago, hello, major, or lawful; g *as in* go, j *as in* age, 'l *as in* rattle; 'n *as in* flatten; ŋ *as in* sing; ch *as in* chalk; sh *as in* show; th *as in* think; *th* as in there; zh *as in* treasure

gazelle (gə•zel') *n.:* small, graceful antelope with large, bright eyes.

girded (gʉrd'id) *v.:* equipped; prepared.

gouging (gouj'iŋ) *v.:* making a groove; scooping out.

grisly (griz'lē) *adj.:* causing horror; horrible.

grovelling (grav'əl•iŋ) *v.:* behaving in a humble or fearful way.

gullies (gul'ēz) *n.:* trenches or ditches caused by running water.

hangings (haŋ'iŋz) *n.:* things hung (as a curtain or tapestry) on the wall.

harken (här'kən) *v.:* to listen carefully.

heedless (hēd'lis) *adj.:* not careful.

hew (hyōō) *v.:* to cut, strike, or chop as with an ax or knife.

homage (häm'ij) *n.:* something done to show honor or respect.

incur (in•kʉr') *v.:* to bring upon oneself.

indignantly (in•dig'nənt•lē) *adv.:* acting with anger because of something that is unfair or not right.

induced (in•dōōst') *v.:* influenced to do something; persuaded.

inhabit (in•hab'it) *v.:* to live in.

inlet (in'let') *n.:* a narrow strip of water leading into the land from another body of water.

invincible (in•vin'sə•bəl) *adj.:* not to be overcome or conquered.

jamb (jam) *n.:* side of a doorway or window.

jest (jest) *n.:* an object of laughter; a joke.

lair (ler) *n.:* den for a wild animal.

landmark (land'•märk') *n.:* an object that identifies a particular place.

leathern (le*th*'ərn) *adj.:* similar to leather.

limbs (limz) *n.:* arms and legs.

lofty (lôf'tē) *adj.:* extremely high.

loomed (lōōmd) *v.:* appeared indistinctly.

lurched (lʉrchd) *v.:* stumbled; staggered.

lured (lōord) *v.:* persuaded; tempted to follow.

magistrates (maj'is•trāts') *n.:* local government officials.

mail (māl) *n.:* small, overlapping rings of metal; armor for the body that is flexible.

maize (māz) *n.:* corn.

mediums (mē'dē•əmz) *n.:* people who are thought by some to communicate with the spirits of the dead.

merits (mer'itz) *n.:* things deserving reward.

mimicked (mim'ikt) *v.:* imitated so as to make fun of.

minstrel (min'strəl) *n.:* travelling singer or storyteller.

mocking (mäk'iŋ) *v.:* making fun of; scorning.

moorlands (moor'landz') *n.:* wide, gently rolling areas of wasteland.

obliged (ə•blījd') *v.:* forced or compelled.

oracle (ôr'ə•kəl) *n.:* place in ancient Greece where the gods were believed to make their wishes known through a priest or priestess.

ought (ôt) *adv.:* at all.

pavilion (pə•vil'yən) *n.:* lightly constructed building in a park.

perceived (pər•sēvd') *v.:* saw; understood.

phenomenal (fə•näm'ə•nəl) *adj.:* very unusual; extraordinary.

pomegranate (päm'gran'it) *n.:* red fruit about the size of an orange with a leathery skin and filled with seeds in red juicy flesh.

privilege (priv'ə•lij) *n.:* a right.

protruding (prō•trōōd'iŋ) *v.:* bulging out.

rampant (ram'pənt) *adj.:* not stopped or checked; spreading wildly.

rapturous (rap'chər•əs) *adj.:* joyous; filled with happiness and joy.

reed (rēd) *n.:* plant growing in wet land.

regulating (reg'yə•lāt'iŋ) *v.:* controlling; adjusting; making sure things run smoothly.

rending (rend'iŋ) *v.:* tearing or ripping violently.

reverberated (ri•vʉr'bə•rāt'əd) *v.:* echoed; resounded.

rushes (rush'iz) *n.:* leaves and stems of plants used to make floor mats.

sari (sä'rē) *n.:* long piece of cloth draped around the body.

scalp lock (skalp läk) *n.:* tuft of hair that remains on the head of a Native American after the head has been shaved.

scowling (skoul'iŋ) *v.:* frowning.

sheer (shir) *adj.:* very steep; almost straight up and down.

shuttle (shut''l) *n.:* device used when weaving to carry threads through the lengthwise threads on the loom.

snares (snerz) *n.:* dangerous or risky traps.

soot (soot) *n.:* black powder left after something burns.

sorcerers (sôr'sər•ərs) *n.:* wizards.

source (sôrs) *n.:* the place where something begins or comes into being.

span (span) *v.:* reach from one side to the other; *n.:* unit of measure equal to nine inches or the distance between the extended thumb and little finger.

spewing (spyōō'iŋ) *v.:* running or gushing out.

sprawling (sprôl'iŋ) *v.:* lying in a spread-out, awkward position.

steed (stēd) *n.:* a lively horse.

stole (stōl) *v.:* moved quietly or silently; took and kept something that belonged to another.

stoved (stovd) *v.:* smashed or broken.

surveyed (sər•vād') *v.:* looked at closely.

tarry (tar'ē) *v.:* stay behind.

tendrils (ten'drəlz) *n.:* thin, leafless parts of a climbing plant that hold the plant by winding around an object.

thither (*th*ith'ər) *adv.:* to that place.

threshold (thresh'ōld') *n.:* entrance.

tilled (tild) *v.:* planted and raised crops.

trident (trīd''nt) *n.:* spear with three prongs or tines, carried as a scepter by the Greek sea god Poseidon.

trophy (trō'fē) *n.:* something taken from an enemy and kept as proof of one's bravery.

unbounded (un•boun'did) *adj.:* having no limits.

valiant (val'yənt) *adj.:* brave.

valor (val'ər) *n.:* courage.

veered (vird) *v.:* went in another direction.

vengeance (ven'jəns) *n.:* hurt or harm done in return for an injury.

vents (vents) *v.:* expresses great feeling.

wiles (wīlz) *n.:* dishonest trick.

wring (riŋ) *v.:* express distress by grasping and twisting (the hands) together.

Acknowledgments

For permission to reprint copyrighted material, grateful acknowledgment is made to the following sources:

Carcanet Press Limited: "Theseus and the Minotaur" from *Greek Gods and Heroes* by Robert Graves. Copyright © 1960 by Robert Graves.

Carus Publishing Company, 30 Grove Street, Suite C, Peterborough, NH 03458: "Isis the Queen" by Robert D. San Souci from *Calliope: Queen of Egypt,* November/December 1991. Copyright © 1991 by Cobblestone Publishing Company. All rights reserved.

The Emma Courlander Trust: "Liongo, a Hero of Shanga" from *The Crest and the Hide and Other African Stories of Heroes, Chiefs, Bards, Hunters, Sorcerers and Common People* by Harold Courlander. Copyright © 1982 by Harold Courlander. "Paul Bunyan's Cornstalk" from *Ride with the Sun: An Anthology of Folk Tales and Stories from the United Nations* by Harold Courlander. Copyright © 1983 by Harold Courlander.

Cricket Magazine: "Rama and the Monkey Host" by Margaret Jones from *Cricket,* vol. 26, no. 4, December 1998. Copyright © 1998 by Margaret Jones.

Doubleday, a division of Random House, Inc.: From *The Power of Myth* by Joseph Campbell and Bill Moyers. Copyright © 1988 by Apostrophe S Productions, Inc. and Bill Moyers and Alfred Van der Marck Editions, Inc. for itself and the estate of Joseph Campbell.

Foreign Languages Press: "The Frog Who Became an Emperor" from *The Peacock Maiden: Folk Tales from China (Third Series).* Copyright © 1958 by Foreign Languages Press.

Fulcrum, Inc.: "The Earth on Turtle's Back" from *Keepers of the Earth: Native American Stories and Environmental Activities for Children* by Michael J. Caduto and Joseph Bruchac. Copyright © 1988, 1989 by Michael J. Caduto and Joseph Bruchac.

Harcourt, Inc.: "Cupid and Psyche" (with American spellings) from *World Tales: The Extraordinary Coincidence of Stories Told in All Times, in All Places* by Idries Shah. Copyright © 1979 by Technographia, S.A. and Harcourt, Inc.

HarperCollins Publishers: From *The Hero Within* by Carol Pearson. Copyright © 1986 by Carol Pearson. "Sun Mother Wakes the World" by Diane Wolkstein. Copyright © 1999, 2003 by Diane Wolkstein.

Hollym International Corporation: "The Herdsman and the Weaver" from *Long Long Time Ago: Korean Folk Tales,* illustrated by Dong-sung Kim. Copyright © 1997 by Hollym Corporation.

Henry Holt and Company, LLC: "Talk" from *The Cow-Tail Switch and Other West African Stories* by Harold Courlander and George Herzog. Copyright © 1947, 1974 by Harold Courlander. "The Little Grey Donkey" from *Buddha Stories* by Demi. Copyright © 1997 by Demi. "The End of the World" from *The Four Corners of the Sky: Creation Stories and Cosmologies from Around the World* by Steve Zeitlin. Copyright © 2000 by Steve Zeitlin.

Houghton Mifflin Company: "The Coming of Evil" and "The Creation of Man" from *Greek Myths* by Olivia Coolidge. Copyright © 1949 and renewed © 1977 by Olivia E. Coolidge. All rights reserved. "The Song of Beowulf" from *Legends of the North* by Olivia E. Coolidge. Copyright © 1951 and renewed © 1979 by Olivia E. Coolidge. All rights reserved.

International African Institute, London: "The Five Helpers" (slightly adapted) from *Tales Told in Togoland* by A. W. Cardinall. "A Man Who Could Transform Himself" from *Akamba Stories* by John S. Mbiti. Copyright © 1966 by Oxford University Press.

Northwestern University Press: "Spider's Bargain with God" from *West African Folk Tales,* translated by Jack Berry, edited and introduced by Richard Spears. Copyright © 1991 by Northwestern University Press.

Octagon Press Limited: "The Alternative," "See What I Mean?" and "There Is More Light Here" from *The Exploits of the Incomparable Mulla Nasrudin* by Idries Shah. Copyright © 1966 by Mulla Nasrudin Enterprises Ltd.; copyright © 1983 by Octagon Press Limited.

Pantheon Books, a division of Random House, Inc.: Adaptations of "Coyote Kills the Giant," "Glooscap Fights the Water Monster" and "The Spirit Wife" from *American Indian Myths and Legends,* edited by Richard Erdoes and Alfonso Ortiz. Copyright © 1984 by Richard Erdoes and Alfonso Ortiz. "The Butterfly" by Chuang Tzu and "Li Chi Slays the Serpent" by Kan Pao from *Chinese Fairy Tales and Fantasies* by Moss Roberts. Copyright © 1979 by Moss Roberts.

G. P. Putnam's Sons, an imprint of Penguin Putnam Books for Young Readers, a division of Penguin Putnam Inc.: "The Snow Woman" from *Mysterious Tales of Japan* by Rafe Martin. Copyright © 1996 by Rafe Martin. All rights reserved.

Random House Children's Books, a division of Random House, Inc.: "Demeter" from *The Random House Book of Greek Myths* by Joan D. Vinge. Copyright © 1999 by Joan D. Vinge.

The Wylie Agency (UK) Ltd.: From *The Literature Machine* by Italo Calvino. Copyright © 1986, 1987 by Secker and Warburg.

University of Oklahoma Press: "Old Man and Old Woman" (retitled "It Is Better To Die Forever"), retold by Chewing Blackbones from *Indian Legends from the Northern Rockies* by Ella E. Clark. Copyright © 1966 by the University of Oklahoma Press.

VAGA, New York: "The Monster Humbaba" from *Gilgamesh: Man's First Story* by Bernarda Bryson. Copyright ©1967 by Holt, Rinehart and Winston; copyright renewed ©1995 by Bernarda Bryson Shahn.

Photo Credits: Page 1, ©2002 ArtToday.com; 3, Bettman/CORBIS; 4, Bettman/CORBIS; 5, The Kobal Collection/TOHO; 6, Christie's Images/CORBIS; 8,9,10, © 2002 ArtToday.com; 13, Historical Picture Archive/CORBIS; 14, Bettmann/CORBIS; 15, Little, Brown and Company, Boston, 1937; 17, AFP/CORBIS; 18, Bettmann/CORBIS; 20, © 2002 ArtToday.com; 22, Chris Rainier/CORBIS; 23, Patrick Ward/CORBIS; 25, 27, 28, 30, © 2002 ArtToday.com; 31 Asian Art & Archaeology, Inc./ CORBIS; 33, © 2002 ArtToday.com; 34, Asian Art & Archaeology/CORBIS; 37 Historical Picture Archive/CORBIS; 39 John Noble/CORBIS; 41, Christel Gerstenberg/CORBIS; 43 George Harrap & Co., London, 1914; 44 © 2002 ArtToday.com; 46, Christel Gerstenberg/CORBIS; 45, Marvel Entertainment; 48, Bettmann/CORBIS; 49, Dover Publications, Inc.; 51, 52, 53, Bettmann/CORBIS; 55, EclectiCollections™; 56, 57, 59, 60 © 2002 ArtToday.com; 63, Gianni Dagli Orti/CORBIS; 64, 66, © 2002 ArtToday.com; 67, Archivo Inconografico, S.A./ CORBIS; 68, Giraudon/Art Resource, NY; 71, Dover Publications, Inc.; 73, Historical Picture Archive/CORBIS; 74, Angelo Hornak/CORBIS; 76, Historical Picture Archive/CORBIS; 77, Victoria Smith/HRW Photo; 79, © 2002 ArtToday.com; 80, Dover Publications, Inc.; 83, Culver Pictures, Inc.; 84, Giraudon/Art Resource, NY; 86, Dudgeon/HRW Photo; 87, The Kobal Collection/Lucasfilm/ 20th Century Fox; 88, AP/Wide World Photos; 90, 91, 92, 93, 94, 95, 96, © 2002 ArtToday.com; 98, Archivo Iconografico, S.A./CORBIS; 100, 102, © 2002 ArtToday.com; 104, The Granger Collection, New York; 105, 106, © 2002 ArtToday.com; 107, Diego Lezama Orezzoli/CORBIS; 109, 110, 112, 114, 115, 117, 118, 120, 122, 124, © 2002 ArtToday.com; 126 Bettmann/CORBIS; 129, © 2002 ArtToday.com; 130, Bridgeman Art Library; 131, Bettmann/ CORBIS; 132, © 2002 ArtToday.com; 135, Christie's Images/CORBIS; 137, 139, 140, 141, 142, 143, 144, 145, © 2002 ArtToday.com; 147, Giraudon/Art Resource, NY; 149, © 2002 ArtToday.com; 150, Bulfinch's Age of Fable or Beauties of Mythology, David McKay, Philadephia, 1898; 151, 152, 153, 155, 157, © 2002 ArtToday.com; 159, Asian Art & Archaeology/CORBIS; 160, 163, 164, 166, 168, 170, 172, © 2002 ArtToday.com; 173, 174, The Granger Collection, New York; 176, © 2002 ArtToday.com; 178, Bettmann/CORBIS; 180, © 2002 ArtToday.com; 182, AKG London; 185, 186, 189, © 2002 ArtToday.com; 190, Catherine Karnow/CORBIS; 192, 195, © 2002 ArtToday.com; 197, Bettmann/CORBIS; 198, Longmans, Green and Co. Ltd., London, 1927; 200, Longmans, Green and Co. Ltd., London, 1927; 202, 205, 207, 209, © 2002 ArtToday.com; 210, Burstein Collection/CORBIS; 212, © 2002 ArtToday.com; 213, Rand McNally & Co., Chicago, 1919; 214, © 2002 ArtToday.com.